Look With
the Heart

Dan Miller

Published by
Phoenix Images
Indianapolis IN

To Steve —
To keep it
alive.

2/01   Pench

Copyright © 1998 by Dan Miller

All rights reserved. No part of this publication may be stored in a retrieval system, or transmitted in any form or by any means, electronic, mechanical, photocopying, recording, or otherwise, either for public or private use, without permission in writing from the publisher, or the author.

Published in Indianapolis, Indiana
By

Phoenix Images
PO Box 531314
Indianapolis, IN 46253-1314

Written by Dan Miller
Cover Design by Paul Chelko

Printed in the United States of America
October, 1997
Triangle Printing Company
4004 Madison Avenue
Indianapolis, IN 46227

Library of Congress Catalog Card Number:
97-76446

Correspondence is Welcome

ISBN 0-9653086-1-8

10 9 8 7 6 5 4 3 2 1
First Edition

For Sandra

who makes my heart sing

Ideas to Think About

Ideas to Think About

WHY I DID THIS

A few years ago I sent a friend some quotes I had collected. After reading them he said, "These quotes are the best expression of you I've ever seen." How, I wondered, could what I hadn't written express me? But then I saw he was right. The quotes I chose to save, why I saved them, what I thought about them, did say a lot about me. And I realized I wanted share my quotes (and myself) with family, friends, and others. The result: **Look With The Heart**.

I started collecting quotes when I was a teenager. (I guess they're really quotations, but I always think of them as quotes.) I can't remember any particular reason for doing it, except I liked them and figured I'd forget them if I didn't cut them out or write them down.

In "The Little Prince," (which inspired my title, **Look With The Heart**,) St. Exupery talks about his first drawing (the one the adults didn't understand.) I have the first quote I ever saved. It came from the New York Times Book Review, and I carried it with me in my wallet for many years. One day I went looking for it and couldn't find it. I remembered it was a poem by G. K. Chesterton, and I remembered what it was about. I looked for it in various Chesterton collections, but it seemed to be gone forever.

Then, a few years ago, my daughter, Lys, was visiting and showed me an old wallet she said I'd given her a long time ago. She thought I'd be interested in the pictures and mementos that were inside. Right. There it was, yellow and wrinkled, but readable. I was thrilled. This is it. It's called "To Grow Straight":

> The splendor of furrowed fields is this: That like all grave
> things they are made straight, and therefore they bend.

> In everything that bows gracefully there must be an effort at
> stiffness.

> Bows are beautiful when they bend only because they try to remain
> rigid, and swordblades can curl like silver ribbons only because
> they are certain to spring straight again.

But the same is true of every tough curve of the tree trunk, of
every strongbacked curve of the bough;

That same thing in nature, that mere droop of weakness, rigidity
yielding a little, like justice swayed by mercy, is the whole
beauty of the earth.

The foil may curve in the lunge, but there is nothing beautiful
about beginning the battle with a crooked foil.

So the strict aim, the strong doctrine, may give a little in the
actual fight with facts.

But that is no reason for beginning with a weak doctrine or a
twisted aim.

Do not be an opportunist; try to be theoretic at all the
opportunities; fate can be trusted to do all the opportunistic
part of it.

Do not try to bend, any more than the trees try to bend.

Try to grow straight, and life will bend you.

So there you have it. My first quote. I wonder how many of us have tried
"To Grow Straight." I wonder how many of us have succeeded.

For me, quotes are more than interesting references to look up from time to
time. They are stimulators that can provoke and inspire new thinking. **Look
With The Heart** is a collection of ideas, and quotes are the medium.

Look With The Heart is not the place to find out what the world's greatest
thinkers have to say about love or children or art or civilization or—
anything. For that there are much better collections.

It is, though, a good launching pad for thought. And it is personal. The
ideas, questions, challenges, issues, that I focus on are those that comprise
much of my thinking, those that I think are important.

I want **Look With The Heart** to be accessible to anyone who is living life in a relatively conscious state. You don't need special qualifications to relate to these ideas. It will help, though, if you are a curious person, open to being stimulated and provoked. Here's a test:

"I could not simplify myself," were the only words written on a suicide note by a character in "Virgin Soil," a Turgenev novel. "I could not simplify myself." If that thought doesn't cause you to pause for a moment—and think—well....

SOME DISCLAIMERS

A few things to 'fess up about:

- If I know the source of a quote, I tell you. If I don't know, I don't say.

- There are many people quoted who are well known. I usually don't attempt to identify them further.

- There are many people quoted of whom I have never heard. I don't attempt to identify them either.

- Sometimes I have seen the same quote attributed to several different people. In those cases I decided who the author should be on the basis of how I felt about it at the moment.

- There is no question that many quotes could be put in different sections than where I've put them. You have my permission to disagree with my choices. You have my permission to cut/rip them out and paste/throw/flush them in a place that makes you happy.

- If you have something to say to me about this book and can't manage to stifle or suppress it, send me an e-mail at dm9888@msn.com.

Dan Miller
October, 1997

BEING ALIVE

I've found many great comments on living life, being alive. They're like looking through a crystal: sometimes I see purple, and then it turns to a cinnamon color; another facet is green, and then there are different kinds of green; and white; and so on. What I see has to do with the colors in the crystal's environment, which, like life, is ever-changing and ever-interesting.

Be as water is, without friction.

Flow around the edges of those within your path.
Surround within your ever-moving depths
   those who come to rest there,
Enfold them, while never for a moment holding on.

Accept whatever distance others are moved within your flow.
Be with them gently, as far as they allow your strength
   to take them,
and fill with your own being the remaining space
   when they are left behind.

When dropping down life's rapids,
Froth and bubble into fragments if you must,
Knowing that the one of your now many
Will just as many times be one again.

And when you've gone as far as you can go,
Quietly await your next beginning.

♦ Author Unknown

Life is a shipwreck, but we must not forget to sing in the boats.

♦ Voltaire

Life breaks us all sometimes,
But some grow strong in broken places.

♦ Ernest Hemingway

I love this next one. It so speaks to living life fully—which we don't do most of the time. Once in a while I'm jolted by an event, usually someone's death, and realize that I'm missing too much because I'm not paying attention, because I'm not really seeing. I've become unaware.

And then, for a while, I pay attention. I notice how beautiful the Golden Gate Bridge is outside my window. I see and smell the flowers that are always here. I see that which surrounds me and has become invisible. I am really alive—for a time.

If I had my life to live all over again, I would pick more Daisies.

If I had my life to live over, I would try to make more mistakes next time, would be sillier than I have been this trip, I would relax. I would limber up.

I know very few things I would take seriously. I would be crazier. I would be less hygienic; I would take more chances; I would take more trips, I would climb more mountains, swim more rivers, and watch more sunsets. I would burn more gasoline. I would eat more ice cream and less beans.

I would have more actual troubles, and fewer imaginary ones. You see, I am one of those people who live prophylactically and sensibly and sanely, hour after hour, day after day.

Oh, I have had my mad moments, and if I had it to do all over again, I would have more of them; in fact, I'd try to have nothing else, just moments, one after another, instead of living so many years ahead.

I have been one of those people who never go anywhere without a thermometer, a hot-water bottle, a gargle, a raincoat and a parachute. If I had it to live all over again I would go places and travel lighter than I have.

If I had my life to live over again, I would start barefoot earlier in the spring, and stay that way later in the fall.

I would play hooky more,
I would ride on more merry-go-rounds,
I'd pick more daisies.

    ♦ An Old Lady

After Ecstasy, the laundry.

    ♦ Zen Saying

For a long time it had seemed to me that life was about to begin, real life, but there was always some obstacle in the way, something to be gotten through first, some unfinished business, time still to be served, a debt to be paid. Then life would begin. At last it dawned on me that the obstacles were my life.

    ♦ Friar Alfred D'Souza

There is no salvation, really, only infinite realms of experience providing more and more tests, demanding more and more faith. When each thing is lived through to the end, there is no death and no regrets, neither is there a false springtime; each moment lived pushes open a wider horizon from which there is no escape save living.

    ♦ Henry Miller

Read that one again. You'll see more the second time—and the third.

People say that what we're all seeking is a meaning for life. I think that what we're seeking is an experience of being alive. No longer do we see life as an adventure to be sought, but rather as a series of dangers to be avoided: drugs, divorce, inflation, cholesterol, nuclear war.

Yet it clearly isn't enough to say 'no' to the things that threaten us if we have nothing worth while to which we care to say 'yes.' Myths can guide, warn, speculate, inform. They are the dreams of the world. Life is the reality. We ignore both at our peril.

◆ Joseph Campbell

Life is what happens while you are making other plans.

◆ Tom Smothers

We should be careful to get out of an experience only the wisdom that is in it—and stop there; lest we be like the cat that sits down on a hot-stove lid. She will never sit down on a hot-stove lid again, and that is well; but also she will never sit down on a cold one any more.

◆ Mark Twain

Experience is not what happens to you, but what you do with what happens to you.

◆ Aldous Huxley

When you have one foot on the dock and one foot in the boat, you wind up with your tush in the water.

◆ Mario Cuomo

The world is a fantasy—so let's find out about it.

♦ Dennis Sciama, English Astrophysicist

Even if you're on the right track, if you just sit there you'll get run over.

♦ Will Rogers

My candle burns at both ends,
It cannot last the night,
But, oh my friends and foes alike,
It gives a lovely light.

♦ Edna St. Vincent Millay

True contentment is a real, even an active, virtue—not only affirmative but creative. It is the power of getting out of any situation all there is in it.

♦ G.K. Chesterton

Chaos breeds life, while order creates habit.

♦ Henry Adams

Life unexamined is not worth living.

♦ Socrates

Be glad for life because it gives you the chance to love and to work and to look up at the stars.

♦ Henry Van Dyke

Life is a game of cards. The hand that is dealt you represents determinism. The way you play it is free will.

♦ Jawaharlal Nehru

Go with it. Every life, according to [Joseph] Campbell, has heroic potential; everyone follows the mythological path from dependency and immaturity to freedom. Campbell's heroism is not to be confused with lust after fame and riches; the most glorious deeds are inner struggles that result in spiritual rebirth.

But he hardly suggests that we find ourselves in the sanctuary of the monastery. "Follow your bliss," Campbell would advise. "Go with it!" Immortality and eternity are now; transcendence and wonder are the stuff of the human condition. "This is the great moment," he told Moyers. "Each incarnation, you might say, has a potentiality, and the mission of life is to live that potentiality."

♦ K. C. Cole

"Immortality and eternity are now." YES! I have more from Joseph Campbell in his "Special" section.

Oh, the experience of this sweet life.

♦ Dante

One must love life before loving its meaning, says Dostoyevsky. Yes, and when love of life disappears, no meaning can console us.

♦ Albert Camus

6

In this world there are only two tragedies. One is not getting what one wants, and the other is getting it.

> ♦ Oscar Wilde

Every man dies, but not every man really lives.

> ♦ "Braveheart" (movie)

One wild, sweet hour of glorious life is worth a world without a name.

> ♦ Author Unknown

Milkman: I know where I'm going.
Guitar: Where?
Milkman: Wherever the party is.

> ♦ Toni Morrison, "Song of Solomon"

Old or young, we're on our last cruise.

> ♦ Robert Louis Stevenson

Most of us wait until we're 65 to become children, and then it's too late.

> ♦ Pablo Picasso

Happy the man, and happy he alone,
He, who can call today his own;
He who, secure within, can say,
Tomorrow do thy worst, for I have lived today.

> ♦ Horace

I would rather be ashes than dust!
I would rather that my
Spark burn out in a brilliant blaze
Than it should be stifled by dry rot.
I would rather be a superb meteor,
Every atom of me in magnificent glow,
Than a sleepy and permanent planet.

The proper function of man is to live,
Not to exist.
I shall not waste my days in trying
To prolong them.
I shall use my time.

◆ Jack London

WHAT'S POSSIBLE

"What's possible" gets everyone's attention: poets, philosophers, scientists, deep thinkers from all disciplines, and the rest of us.

Those who contemplate "possibility" point us in a direction that, while unfamiliar, can have great, unpredictable payoffs. They want us to confront our fear of the unknown and the untried and not be deterred.

At the same time there are no real road maps, helpful hints or how to's to guide us on the journey. I like the whole process because it takes me beyond my comfort zone, out of the boredom and beyond certainty into—who knows what? Living a life of possibility is its own reward.

If seed in the black earth
Can turn into such beautiful roses,
What might not the heart of man become
In its long journey toward the stars.

   ♦ G.K. Chesterton

A human being is a part of the whole, called by us "universe," a part limited in time and space. He experiences himself, his thoughts and feelings as something separated from the rest—a kind of optical delusion of his consciousness. This delusion is a kind of prison for us, restricting us to our personal desires and to affection for a few persons nearest to us. Our task must be to free ourselves from this prison by widening our circle of compassion to embrace all living creatures and the whole of nature in its beauty.

   ♦ Albert Einstein

Imagination is more important than knowledge.

   ♦ Albert Einstein

9

On this mountain
the Lord of hosts
will provide
for all peoples
juicy, rich food
and pure choice wines.
On this mountain
he will destroy
the veil that veils
all peoples.

> ♦ The Prophet Isaiah

She knew there was something she was missing and she ached to be able to communicate beyond the few words she knew. It was obvious to her that the people of the clan understood more than the simple words, but she just didn't know how.

The problem was she didn't "see" the hand signals. They were random movements to her, not purposeful motion. She simply hadn't been able to grasp the concept of talking with movement. That it was even possible had never occurred to her. It was totally beyond her realm of experience.

> ♦ Jane Auel, "Clan of the Cave Bear"

If we all worked on the assumption that what is accepted as true is really true, there would be little hope of advance.

> ♦ Orville Wright

The reasonable man adapts himself to the conditions that surround him. The unreasonable man adapts the surrounding conditions to himself.

> ♦ George Bernard Shaw

To believe what has not occurred in history will not occur at all,
Is to argue disbelief in the dignity of man.

♦ Mahatma Gandhi

In this age of wonders
things undreamed of are daily being seen,
the impossible is ever becoming possible.

♦ Mahatma Gandhi

Man would not have attained the possible unless time and again he had not
reached out for the impossible.

♦ Max Weber

The only way to discover the limits of the possible is to go beyond them to
the impossible.

♦ Arthur C. Clarke

Only those willing to go too far know how far they can really go.

♦ Chuck Yaeger

Interesting, Max, Arthur, and Chuck, how much you guys think alike. Hum!

The important thing is this:
To be able at any moment
To sacrifice what we are
For what we could become.

♦ Charles DuBois

All the experts are experts on what was, there are no experts on what will be.

♦ David Ben Gurion

If I were to wish for anything, I should not wish for wealth and power, but for the passionate sense of what might be, for the eye, which, ever young and ardent, sees the possible. Pleasure disappoints, possibility never. And what wine is so sparkling, what so fragrant, what so intoxicating as possibility.

♦ Soren Kierkegaard

Two stone cutters were observed, each working on a slab of marble. A passer-by, curious, asked the first what he was doing, "I am chipping away at this marble," he replied. Coming upon the second, he posed the same question, "can't you see?" he replied, "I am building a cathedral."

One stone cutter saw something different. In front of him was not a block of marble but a possibility—a vision that inspired him—a future work of art. His time wasn't spent in getting the job done, but in expressing, through the stone, what wasn't yet but could be. His work was not mere labor, but an act of discovery, of dedication, of bringing into being.

Each one of us faces a similar choice: the opportunity to spend our time chipping away at the stones that appear before us—or to set ourselves to the task of creating new possibilities, carving new realities, from the raw material that our lives present.

♦ Werner Erhard

Can we observe what everyone observes;
and think what no one has thought?

♦ Albert Svens Gorke

1) What is defined as impossible today is impossible only in the context of the present paradigm.

2) Every creative act involves...a new innocence of perception, liberated from the cataract of accepted belief.

- Arthur Koestler

"The cataract of accepted belief." Koestler knows how to get my attention.

Most people look at what is and never see what can be.

- Author Unknown

Most humans, in varying degrees, are already dead. They have lost their dreams, their ambitions. They have surrendered their fight for self-esteem and compromised their great potential. They have settled for a life of mediocrity. Yet, they can each perform the greatest miracle. They can each come back from the dead.

- O.G. Mandino, "The Greatest Miracle in the World"

What is thinkable is also possible.

- Ludwig Wittgenstein

Nothing will ever be attempted if all possible objections must first be overcome.

- Samuel Johnson

Treat a man as he is and he will remain as he is. Treat a man as he can and should be and he will become as he can and should be.

♦ Goethe

IN THE ARENA

I often talk about the difference between watching the game from the stands and being down on the playing field playing the game. Playing the game totally alters your perspective, your sense of making a difference, your responsibility for the outcome and your relationship to the team. In life, being on the playing field is the most satisfying place to be.

Let no one be discouraged by the belief that there is nothing that one man or one woman can do against the enormous array of the world's ills, against the misery and ignorance, injustice and violence.

Few have the greatness to bend history itself, but each of us can work to change a small portion of the events, and in the total of all those acts will be written the history of this generation. It is from numberless, diverse acts of courage and belief that human history is shaped.

Each time a man stands up for an ideal, or acts to improve the lot of others, or strikes out against injustice, he sends forth a tiny ripple of hope. And crossing each other from a million different centers of energy and daring, those ripples build a current which can sweep down the mightiest walls of oppression and resistance.

♦ Robert F. Kennedy

Seek, above all, for a game worth playing. Having found the game, play it with intensity—play as if your life and sanity depended on it. Follow the example of the French existentialists and flourish a banner bearing the word "engagement."

♦ Robert S. Deroop

The man who, being really on the way, falls upon hard times in the world will not, as a consequence turn to that friend who offers him refuge and comfort and encourages his old self to survive. Rather, he will seek out someone who will faithfully and inexorably help him to risk himself, so that he may endure the suffering and pass courageously through it, thus making of it a "raft that leads to the far shore."

Only to the extent that man exposes himself over and over again to annihilation can that which is indestructible arise within him. In this lies the dignity of daring.

Thus the aim of practice is not to develop an attitude which allows a man to acquire a state of harmony and peace wherein nothing can ever trouble him. On the contrary, practice should teach him to let himself be assaulted, perturbed, moved, insulted, broken and battered—that is to say that should enable him to dare to let go his futile hankering after harmony, surcease from pain and a comfortable life in order that he may discover, in doing battle with the forces that oppose him that which awaits him beyond the world of opposites.

The first necessity is that we should have the courage to face life and to encounter all that is most perilous in the world.

Only if we venture repeatedly through zones of annihilations can our contact with Divine Being which is beyond annihilation become firm and stable.

♦ Karlfried Graf von Durckheim

Satisfaction comes when ones thoughts and ones actions are the same.

♦ Jawaharlal Nehru

In a democracy, agreement is not essential but participation is.

♦ Motto: World Affairs Council

It is not the critic who counts, not the man who points out how the strong man stumbled or where the doer of deeds could have done better.

The credit belongs to the man who is actually in the arena; whose face is marred by dust and sweat and blood; who strives valiantly; who errs and comes short again and again; who knows the great enthusiasms, the great devotions, and spends himself in a worthy cause; who, at the best, knows in the end the triumph of high achievement; and who, at the worst, if he fails, at least fails while daring greatly, so that his place shall never be with those cold and timid souls who know neither victory nor defeat.

♦ Theodore Roosevelt

I had a hard time figuring out where to put the history that follows. It could just as easily have gone in "Taking a Risk," or "Breaking Through," or "What Do You Stand For," or "I Declare," or "What are the Odds?" Obviously, the qualities called for in those sections are appropriate for this man:

Lost his job in 1832
Defeated for the Legislature in 1832
Failed in business in 1833
Elected to Legislature in 1834
Sweetheart died in 1835
Had nervous breakdown in 1836
Defeated for Speaker in 1838
Defeated for nomination for Congress in 1843
Elected to Congress in 1846
Rejected for Land Office in 1849
Defeated for Senate in 1854
Defeated for nomination for Vice President in 1856
Again defeated for the Senate in 1858
But...

In 1860 Abraham Lincoln was elected President of the United States

As to those for whom to work hard, to begin and begin again, to attempt and be mistaken, to go back and rework everything from top to bottom, and still find reason to hesitate from one step to the next—as to those, in short, for whom to work in the midst of uncertainty and apprehension is tantamount to failure, all I can say is that clearly we are not from the same planet.

♦ Michel Foucault

In the struggle for justice, the only reward is the opportunity to be in the struggle.

♦ Frederick Douglass

BEYOND BEYOND

Sometimes I hear or read something that stretches me beyond where my thinking has allowed me to go. It's a challenge to confront what is being pointed at. It's also fun to play in the unknown.

Touch is only possible at the edge of spaces
Light is only precious during dark intervals

♦ Keith Jarrett

My propositions serve as elucidations in the following way: anyone who understands me eventually recognizes them as nonsensical, when he has used them—as steps—to climb up beyond them. He must, so to speak, throw away the ladder after he has climbed up it.

He must surmount these propositions, then he sees the world rightly. Whereof one cannot speak, thereof one must be silent.

♦ Ludwig Wittgenstein

Time does not end.
Because the circle is not round.

♦ From the Macedonian movie, "Before the Rain"

Do we decide questions at all? We decide answers no doubt, but surely the questions decide us.

♦ Lewis Carroll

(now the ears of my ears awake and
 now the eyes of my eyes are opened)

◆ e.e. cummings

The sun is new each day.
Every day is like every other.

◆ Heraclitus, Greek Philosopher

Rest in the riddle.

◆ Robert Graves

Everything we see could also be otherwise.
Everything we can describe at all could also be otherwise.

◆ Ludwig Wittgenstein

A man's at odds to know his mind cause his mind is aught he has to know it
with. He can know his heart, but he dont want to. Rightly so. Best not to
look in there.

◆ Cormac McCarthy, "Blood Meridian"

Tell us, they'll say to me. So we will understand and be able to resolve
things. They'll be mistaken. It's only the things you don't understand that
you can resolve. There will be no resolution.

◆ Peter Hoeg, "Smilla's Sense of Snow"

Lie awake in the big city and you can hear it like the beady scrape of cricket wings in the Miami night—the nasal insect drill of need and neurosis.

Insects are what neurosis would sound like, if neurosis could make a noise with its nose.

♦ Martin Amis, "The Information"

JUST FOR FUN

I notice that baseball people have a lot of funny things to say. But even though Casey and Yogi stand out, they're not alone.

There's a time in every man's life, and I've had plenty of 'em.

    ♦ Casey Stengel

All right, everybody line up alphabetically according to your height.

    ♦ Casey Stengel

I made up my mind, but I made it up both ways.

    ♦ Casey Stengel

It's easy to get good players. Gettin' 'em to play together, that's the hard part.

    ♦ Casey Stengel

Most people my age are dead at the present time.

    ♦ Casey Stengel

I heard it can't be done, but it don't always work.

    ♦ Casey Stengel

98% of hitting is mental. The other half is physical.

♦ Yogi Berra

I really didn't say half the things I've said.

♦ Yogi Berra

When you come to a fork in the road, take it.

♦ Yogi Berra

You can observe a lot just by watching.

♦ Yogi Berra

The future ain't what it used to be.

♦ Yogi Berra

The sun don't shine on the same dog's ass every afternoon.

♦ Jim (Catfish) Hunter

Did you ever get the feeling that the world is a tuxedo and you're a pair of brown shoes?

♦ George Gobel

The advantage of being bisexual is that it increases the chances of you getting a date on Saturday night.

♦ Woody Allen

Just because they're yelling at you doesn't mean you're wrong.

♦ Richie Garcia, Baseball Umpire

I am the Emperor of Paranoia. I am more schizophrenic than everyone. I'm so paranoid that I fear every new patient who comes here will be more paranoid than me, and I'll lose my title.

♦ Garces, Mental Institution Patient

Before I speak, I have something important to say.

♦ Groucho Marx

A man is standing in his yard throwing corn. A passer-by asks him why, and he replies, "Because it keeps the tigers away." "But there aren't any tigers here," the passer-by protests. "Well, it works then, doesn't it?" the man says.

♦ Sufi Parable

I used to be Snow White, but I drifted.

♦ Mae West

THE SPIRITUAL YOU

I had a hard time naming this section. When I say spiritual or spirituality I know that for many people religious connotations come to mind first. That isn't the way it is for me. The ecclesiastical can be included, but I want to convey more the metaphysical, the nonphysical, that which is related to the higher emotions or to the aesthetic senses.

Having said that, the first quote below has to do with God and church. Go figure.

Tell the truth, have you ever found God in church? I never did. I just found a bunch of folks hoping for him to show. Any God I ever felt in church I brought in with me. And I think all the other folks did too. They came to church to share God, not find God.

♦ Alice Walker, "The Color Purple"

We have met on the plane of imagination where it is indeed possible to share everything we have come to be.

♦ Arthur Miller

Walk tall as the trees; live strong as the mountains; be gentle as the spring winds; keep the warmth of summer in your heart, and the Great Spirit will always be with you.

♦ Native American Chant

That is happiness, to be dissolved into something complete and great.

♦ Willa Cather

One of the main ideas of the 20th century spiritual teacher G.I. Gurdjieff was that the search for self-knowledge and inner development can take place—and for most modern people must take place—in the midst of ordinary life.

♦ Jacob Needleman, "Money & the Meaning of Life"

We are not human beings having a spiritual experience. We are spiritual beings having a human experience.

♦ Teilhard de Chardin

With an eye made quiet by the power
Of harmony, and the deep power of joy,
We see into the life of things.

♦ William Wordsworth

If, as Herod, we fill our lives with things, and again with things...
If we consider ourselves so unimportant that we must fill every moment of
    our lives with action,
When will we have the time to make the long, slow journey across the desert
    as did the Magi?
Or sit and watch the stars as did the shepherds?
Or brood over the coming of the child as did Mary?
For each of us, there is a desert to travel.
A star to discover.
And a being within ourselves to bring to life.

♦ Author Unknown

God dwells where man lets him in.

♦ Martin Buber

FOR SPECIAL ATTENTION:

"THE HEART AROUSED" by DAVID WHYTE

"The Heart Aroused" is subtitled "Poetry and the Preservation of the Soul in Corporate America." *Whyte is extraordinary. He's a poet, an interpreter of poetry, and a management consultant who brings poetry and soul to the business world—to rave reviews.*

That I devote two sections to his work is evidence of how much I think of him. He is an elegant and eloquent speaker.

In the middle of the road of my life
I awoke in a dark wood
Where the true way was wholly lost.
Ah, how hard a thing it is to tell what a wild, and rough, and stubborn wood
    this is,
Which in my thought renews the fear!

> ♦ Dante, "Divine Comedy"

Despite everything you have achieved, life refuses to grant you, and always will refuse to grant you, immunity from its difficulties.

Becoming aware of this after a lifetime of accepting success as the ultimate healing balm, as something that will give you protection, is, declares Dante, like waking in a dark wood. He begins by admitting that the human mind never sees success as "here," but always ahead, down the road.

He says that the day when you have your desk finally cleared will not arrive. That the level of safety you are aiming for on the corporate ladder is an illusion. He says the child you have at home, for whom you are making many sacrifices, will be grown and gone by the time you struggle back through the traffic.

> ♦ David Whyte

Confronted with the difficulty and drama of work, we look into our lives as we look into deep water. We kneel, as if by the side of a pool, seeing in one moment not only the fleeting and gossamer reflection of our own face, clouded and disturbed by every passing breath and the lives of all the innumerable creatures that live in its waters, but the hidden depths below, beyond our sight, sustaining and holding everything we comprehend.

◆ David Whyte

If a fool would persist in his folly, he would become wise.

◆ William Blake

I should be content
to look at a mountain
for what it is
and not as a comment on my life.

◆ David Ignatow

We are continually hiding our light under a bushel because we feel safer that way

◆ David Whyte

If we can see the path ahead laid out for us, there is a good chance it is not our path; it is probably someone else's we have substituted for our own.

◆ David Whyte

They named the huge one Grendel:
If he had a father no one knew him,
Or whether there'd been others before these two,
Hidden evil before hidden evil.
They live in secret places, windy
Cliffs, wolf dens where water pours
From the rocks, then runs underground, where mist
Steams like black clouds, and the groves of trees
Growing out over their lake are all covered
With frozen spray, and wind down snake-like
Roots that reach as far as the water
And help keep it dark. At night that lake
Burns like a torch. No one knows its bottom,
No wisdom reaches such depths. A deer,
Hunted through the woods by packs of hounds,
A stag with great horns, though driven through the forest
From faraway places, prefers to die
On those shores, refuses to save its life
In that water. It isn't far, nor is it
A pleasant spot!

♦ Beowulf

Beowulf mortally wounds Grendel who then staggers back to die in the mere. That night there is tremendous feasting and gift giving. The problem, it seems, has been solved in one swift movement. But that night, as Beowulf sleeps with his men in a different hall, something else comes from the swamp to Herot, fights off the best warriors, and retreats with its human victim. Grendel's mother.

The message in this portion of the poem is unsparing. It is not the thing you fear that you must deal with, it is the mother of the thing you fear. The very thing that has given birth to the nightmare.

We are being told that Grendel's mother is the living incarnation of our disowned side, which has been forced to live in unfamiliar places, the fading-moon portion of ourselves, the part of us that refused to show our limp.

♦ David Whyte

Last night as I was sleeping
I dreamt—marvelous error!
that I had a beehive
here inside my heart.
And the golden bees
were making white combs
and sweet honey
from my old failures.

♦ Antonio Machado

And the spark behind fear
recognized as life
leaps into flame

Always this energy smolders inside
when it remains unlit
the body fills with dense smoke.

♦ David Whyte

The Greeks said that if the gods really wanted to punish someone, they granted that person everything they had wished for.

♦ David Whyte

Ten years ago . . .
I turned my face for a moment

and it became my life.

♦ Anonymous woman who sacrificed her sacred desires and personal visions on the altar of work and success

NOTHING STAYS THE SAME

While it is true that we repeat the past (see "The Past Lives On" and "Whatever Goes Around Comes Around") it is also true that we're always in the midst of change. I am not going to resolve this seeming paradox; you're on your own. I am, however, going to provide some quotes.

Every 24 hours the world turns over for the guy who was sitting on top of it.

♦ Sparky Anderson, Baseball Manager

You ask how we got here. Baby, don't ask how, cause that was some time other than now.

♦ John Hiatt

The world is changing faster than we can change ourselves or our political or social institutions. We are living in a revolutionary period, in which everything is on ball bearings.

♦ James Reston

For we live not in a settled and finished world, but in one which is going on.

♦ John Dewey, "Democracy & Education"

Today's peacock is tomorrow's feather duster.

♦ Arthur Martinez, CEO, Sears

We must be clear-sighted in beginnings, for, as in their budding we discern not the danger, so in their full growth we perceive not the remedy.

♦ Montaigne, "Essays"

HIT THE PAUSE BUTTON:

SERGE KAHILI KING

From time to time I'll "Hit the Pause Button." It will be a short "time out" to focus on some idiosyncratic material that amuses or interests me. Now, the fact is I could have added these "Pauses" to the "For Special Attention" or "Just Because I Like Them" sections, but I thought there were already enough of those, so . . .

I learned about Serge Kahili King *and his books,* "Seeing is Believing," *and* "Winning With Love," *in Kauai, one of my favorite places in the world. They say he is the adopted grandson of a Hawaiian kahuna from the "kapua" or shaman tradition. His work reflects that tradition.*

He talks about the "Aloha Spirit," and points out that aloha stands for much more than just "hello" or "goodbye" or "love." Its deeper meaning is "the joyful (oha) sharing (alo) of life energy (ha) in the present (alo)."

The Aloha Philosophy:

1. **IKE:** The World Is What You Think It Is
2. **KALA:** There Are No Limits
3. **MAKIA:** Energy Flows Where Attention Goes
4. **MANAWA:** Now Is The Moment Of Power
5. **ALOHA:** To Love Is To Be Happy With
6. **MANA:** All Power Comes From Within
7. **PONO:** Effectiveness Is The Measure Of Truth

35

Most people can stay motivated for two or three months. A few people can stay motivated for two or three years. But a winner will stay motivated for as long as it takes to win.

   ♦ Art Williams

There are no obstacles on the road of life...only road conditions.

You can't control the wind, but you can always adjust your sail.

People don't fail, plans do. People just give up or make new plans.

"Guiding" is when one identifies with or becomes the person to be healed and then heals oneself.

INTEGRITY

Here I'm talking about a special kind of "integrity," more a completeness, a wholeness. So when one part is missing, integrity is missing, the whole is no longer whole. Something essential is lacking.

Instinctively we know when integrity is missing, but too often we choose to overlook it. When we compromise our integrity we always pay a price. At a minimum we should be aware of what we're doing.

The society which scorns plumbing because plumbing is a humble activity and tolerates shoddiness in philosophy because it is an exalted activity will have neither good plumbing nor good philosophy. Neither its pipes nor its theories will hold water.

♦ John W. Gardner, "Excellence"

In answer to the question, "why doesn't Gandhi need notes when he makes a speech," Desai (Gandhi's secretary) said, "what Gandhi thinks, feels, says and does, are all the same so he never has to remember anything."

♦ Author Unknown

Who's copying whom here?

If you tell the truth, you don't have to remember anything.

♦ Mark Twain

We live in one world and each act affects the whole.

♦ Corita Kent

I do the best I know how, the very best I can; and I mean to keep right on doing it to the end. If the end brings me out all right, what is said against me will not amount to anything. If the end brings me out all wrong, then angels swearing I was right would make no difference.

♦ Abraham Lincoln

Insights emerge not chiefly because they are intellectually true or even because they are helpful, but because they have a certain form that is beautiful because it completes what is incomplete in us.

♦ Rollo May

I debated whether to put this next one someplace else. You figure out why I didn't move it.

If you put on the garb of a dog, you must bark like one.

♦ South Indian Proverb

If I were two-faced, would I be wearing this one?

♦ Abraham Lincoln

FOR SPECIAL ATTENTION :

CHINESE INSPIRATION

I don't think the Chinese have a corner on poetic beauty, but what I have come across is extraordinary.

Screened by the trees the sound of the brook is a soft jingle;
To welcome us the birds sing in a chatter.
Together we have penetrated the quiet path along the winding stream;
I for you collect berries,
You bedeck my hair with blossoms.

Anon we sit together on the water-brink,
With a tree to shade the haughty sun.
Deep in talk we reck naught of the evening rooks:
At this hour there are only you and I,
And what room is there for them?

    ♦ Hu Shih

Thirty spokes unite at the wheels hub:
It is the center hole that makes it useful.
Shape clay into a vessel;
It is the space within that makes it useful.
Cut out the doors and windows for a room;
It is the holes which make it useful.
Therefore profit comes from what is there;
Usefulness from what is not there.

    ♦ Lao Tzu

There is no need to run outside
For better seeing,
Nor to peer from a window. Rather abide
At the center of your being . . .
Search your heart and see . . .
The way to do is to be.

     ♦ Lao Tze

Why are you unhappy?
Because 99.9% of what you think,
And everything you do,
Is for your self,
And there isn't one.

     ♦ Wu Wei Wu

In order to contract a thing, one should surely expand it first.
In order to weaken, one will surely strengthen first.
In order to overthrow, one will surely exalt first.
In order to take, one will surely give first.
This is called subtle wisdom.

     ♦ Lao Tzu

HEROES

Heroes come in many guises. Regrettably, since most real heroes never get their 15 minutes of fame, unless we're looking for them we probably miss them. We usually look for flaws, for what's wrong with people, rather than for their courage, their nobility, their greatness. We ought to change what we look for.

Your action, ladies and gentlemen, in giving me this honor, has brought to my mind a very simple and homely simile. Have you noticed what happens when you try to point out something to your dog? He does not look in the direction you are pointing, but at your outstretched hand and finger.

I cannot help thinking that you are acting in a somewhat similar way in paying so much attention to me. I am pointing—as I have never ceased to point for the past forty years—to someone outside myself. And you are saying in effect "What a handsome finger she has! And what a beautiful ring she is wearing!"

The highest honor and the deepest gratitude you can pay me is to turn your attention from me to the direction in which I am pointing—to The Child.

♦ Maria Montessori

We're not in this to test the waters. We are in this to make waves.

♦ Author Unknown

A man goes to knowledge as he goes to war, wide awake, with fear, with respect and with absolute assurance. Going to knowledge or going to war in any other manner is a mistake, and whoever makes it will live to regret his steps.

♦ Carlos Castaneda, "The Teachings of Don Juan"

The answer to helplessness is not so very complicated. A man can do something for peace without having to jump into politics. Each man has inside him a basic decency and goodness. If he listens to it and acts on it he is giving a great deal of what the world needs most. It's not complicated, but it takes courage. It takes courage for a man to listen to his own goodness and to act on it. Dare we, do we dare be ourselves? This is the question that counts.

♦ Pablo Casals

Courage is willingness to get up after you've been knocked down. You have to consider the staying condition of the person. That's the real yardstick of courage, that bounce-back resilience. You have to take the buffeting. And you have to rise from that fallen position feeling whole rather than battered.

♦ Rachel Robinson, Widow of Jackie Robinson

Forget about likes and dislikes. They are of no consequence. Just do what must be done. This may not be happiness, but it is greatness.

♦ George Bernard Shaw

A hero is no braver than an ordinary man, but he is brave five minutes longer.

♦ Ralph Waldo Emerson

Heroes are ordinary men and women who dare to see and meet the call of a possibility bigger than themselves. Breakthroughs are created by heroes, by men and women who will stand for the result while it is still only a possibility—people willing to create the path to the result while others are still squabbling about the right path and arguing about right answers— people who will act to make possibility real.

♦ Werner Erhard

In our Indian stories and our Indian epics it is always said that the great man should be a man devoted to action and yet above action, not controlled by action but controlling action and remaining himself, whether victory comes or defeat.

♦ Jawaharlal Nehru

From the creation of the world, it has been customary for the result to come last. If one would truly learn anything from great actions, one must pay attention precisely to the beginning. In case one who should act were to judge himself according to the result, he would never get to the point of beginning. Even though the result may give joy to the whole world, it cannot help the hero, for he would get to know the result only when the whole thing was over, and it was not by this he became a hero, but he was such for the fact that he began.

♦ Soren Kierkegaard, "Fear and Trembling"

Courage is mastery of fear—not absence of fear.

♦ Mark Twain

Heroism is first and foremost the courage to see in time.

♦ Author Unknown

Success is never final,
Failure is never fatal,
It's the courage that counts.

♦ Winston Churchill

Cowards die many times before their death.

♦ William Shakespeare, "Julius Caesar"

Frank O'Connor, the Irish writer, tells in one of his books how as a boy, he and his friends would make their way across the countryside and when they came to an orchard wall that seemed too high and too doubtful to try and too difficult to permit their voyage to continue they took off their hats and tossed them over the wall—and then they had no choice but to follow them.

♦ John F. Kennedy

Only a few achieve the colossal task of holding together without being split asunder, the clarity of their vision alongside an ability to take their place in a materialistic world. They are the modern heroes. Artists at least have a form within which they can hold their own conflicting opposites together. But there are some who have no recognized artistic form that serve this purpose, they are artists of the living. To my mind these last are the supreme heroes in our soulless society.

♦ Irene Claremont de Castillejo

Without belittling the courage with which men have died, we should not forget those acts of courage with which men have lived. The courage of life is often a less dramatic spectacle than the courage of a final moment, but it is no less a magnificent mixture of triumph and tragedy. A man does what he must—in spite of personal consequences, in spite of obstacles, dangers and pressures—and that is the basis of all human morality.

♦ John F. Kennedy

One man with courage makes a majority.

♦ Andrew Jackson

Courage is grace under pressure.

♦ Ernest Hemingway

Superstars strive for approbation; heroes walk alone. Superstars crave consensus; heroes define themselves by the judgment of a future they see it as their task to bring about. Superstars seek success in a technique for eliciting support; heroes pursue success as the outgrowth of inner values.

♦ Henry Kissinger

He who thinks of the consequences cannot be brave.

♦ Ingush Proverb

I ALREADY KNOW THAT

The most difficult people I've worked with (or known for that matter) are those who know a lot—or think they do. The arrogance and closed-mindedness associated with knowledge is maddening. Sometimes the arrogance has to do with the number of degrees one has. At other times it is related to looking down on the rest of us because of the position one holds. Often it is a defensive posture to deflect being challenged by others.

I also know a lot of brilliant people who aren't in love with their knowledge. They, I think, are wise, not just smart.

What we know is a drop,
What we don't know is an ocean.

    ♦ Isaac Newton

What you learn after you know everything is what really counts.

    ♦ John Wooden

It is impossible for anyone to begin to learn that which he thinks he already knows.

    ♦ Epictetus

A learned blockhead is a greater blockhead than an ignorant one.

    ♦ Benjamin Franklin

The greatest wisdom is knowing that your wisdom is too late. You understand everything when there is no longer anything to understand.

◆ Umberto Eco, "Foucault's Pendulum"

Discoveries of any great moment in mathematics and other disciplines, once they are discovered, are seen to be extremely simple and obvious, and make everybody, including their discoverer, appear foolish for not having discovered them before. It is all too often forgotten that the ancient symbol for prenascence of the world is a fool, and that foolishness, being a divine state, is not a condition to be either proud or ashamed of.

Unfortunately we find systems of education today that have departed so far from the plain truth that they now teach us to be proud of what we know and ashamed of ignorance. This is doubly corrupt. It is not only because pride is in itself a mortal sin, but also to teach pride in knowledge is to put an effective barrier against any advance upon what is already known, since it makes one ashamed to look beyond the bonds imposed by one's ignorance.

To any person prepared to enter with respect into the realm of his great and universal ignorance, the secrets of being will eventually unfold, and they will do so in a measure according to his freedom from natural and indoctrinated shame in his respect of their revelation.

In the face of the strong, and indeed violent, social pressures against it, few people have been prepared to take this simple and satisfying course toward sanity.

◆ G. Spencer Brown

Whoever undertakes to set himself up as a judge of truth and knowledge is shipwrecked by the laughter of the gods.

◆ Albert Einstein

There is, it seems to us at best, only a limited value in the knowledge derived from experience. The knowledge imposes a pattern, and falsifies, for the pattern is new in every moment and every moment is a new and shocking valuation of all we have been.

◆ T.S. Eliot

How can we remember our ignorance, which our growth requires, when we are using our knowledge all the time?

◆ Henry David Thoreau

Intelligence is not how much we know how to do,
But how we behave when we don't know what to do.

◆ John Holt

No matter what happens, there is always somebody who knew that it would.

◆ Damon Runyon

The more we live by our intellect, the less we understand the meaning of life.

◆ Leo Tolstoy

A new idea is first condemned as ridiculous
And then dismissed as trivial
Until finally it becomes what everybody knows

◆ William James

J: We Japanese do not think it strange if a dialogue leaves undefined what is really intended, or even restores it back to the keeping of the undefinable.

I: That is part, I believe, of every dialogue that has turned well between thinking beings. As if of its own accord, it can take care that that undefinable something not only does not slip away, but displays its gathering force ever more luminously in the course of the dialogue.

J: Our dialogues with the Count probably failed to turn out so well. We younger men challenged him much too directly to satisfy our thirst for handy information.

I: Thirst for knowledge and greed for explanations never lead to a thinking inquiry.

 ♦ Martin Heidegger

I have less and less tolerance with jerks who make a career out of criticizing. Critical thinking is great. An ax to grind or cheap shots for the sake of being clever or sounding smart annoys me. Change the channel when they're on TV. Tear up their papers. Don't buy their books. Something. James L. Adams *says it more elegantly:*

The judgment of ideas, unfortunately, is an extremely popular and rewarded pastime. One finds more newspaper space devoted to judgment (critic columns, political analyses, editorials, etc.) than to the creation of ideas.

In the university, much scholarship is devoted to judgment, rather than creativity. One finds that people who heap negative criticism upon all ideas they encounter are often heralded for their practical sense and sophistication. Bad-mouthing every else's concepts is in fact a cheap way to attempt to demonstrate your own mental superiority.

And now, comments on the arrogance of anti-knowledge:

Rarely do we find men who willingly engage in hard solid thinking. There is an almost universal quest for easy answers and half-baked solutions. Nothing pains some people more than having to think.

♦ Martin Luther King, Jr.

Anything little known is assumed to be wonderful.

♦ Tacitus

JUST BECAUSE I LIKE THEM

What's the difference between the diplomat and the military man? The answer is they both do nothing, but the military get up very early in the morning and do it with great discipline, while the diplomats do it late in the afternoon, in utter confusion.

♦ Vernon Walters, Former General & US Ambassador to the UN

Fool me once, shame on you;
Fool me twice, shame on me.

♦ Jim Selman

Two samples from the Bulwer-Lytton fiction contest *for bad writing:*

The sun hiccuped morning onto the weeping landscape as Cassandra lay on her great four poster, one arm across her forehead, the other—soon to snap forward to pick up the alarm clock she so abhorred and hurl it through the leaded bay window of her bedroom onto the pristine green of her garden below (the sound of which would no doubt, as it did every morning, awaken the ancient butler, an old man who had worked for the family ever since its tea-planting days in far-off Sri Lanka, formerly Ceylon)—lying gracefully by her side, white and ivory.

She was like the driven snow beneath the galoshes of my lust.

If you don't know where you're going,
Any road will get you there.

♦ M. N. Chatterjee

Man's capacity for justice makes democracy possible;
but man's inclination to injustice makes democracy necessary.

♦ Reinhold Niebuhr

An acquaintance of Dr. Johnson encouraged him to visit a remote site in Ireland with the assurance, "Tis truly worth seeing." "Worth seeing perhaps, sir," Johnson replied tartly, "but not worth going to see."

♦ Author Unknown

God provides the wind, but man must raise the sails.

♦ St. Augustine

The winds of grace are always blowing, but you've got to raise the sail.

♦ Ramakrishna

Hum . . .!!

Some of you men sure do make me tired.
You got a mouthful of "gimme,"
And a handful of "much obliged."

♦ Bessie Smith

I think most of us are looking for a calling, not a job. Most us, like the assembly line worker, have jobs that are too small for our spirit. Jobs are not big enough for people.

♦ Nora Watson, in Studs Terkel's book, "Working"

Babe Ruth struck out 1,330 times.

> ♦ Plaque on President Reagan's desk

The test of a first rate intelligence is the ability to hold two opposed ideas in the mind at the same time, and still retain the ability to function.

> ♦ F. Scott Fitzgerald

After spending much of my life advocating a significant public sector role in our lives, I have defected. I have joined those of you for whom government is more an annoyance than a help. It would be great if we had a political alternative that represents both economic sanity and social conscience. In the meantime, I say less, not more, government:

Bureaucracy is a process which converts energy into solid waste.

> ♦ Author Unknown

Oliver Wendell Holmes tells one on himself after boarding a train without his ticket:

Conductor: Never mind about the ticket, Mr. Justice, I trust you.
Holmes: I know you trust me, but I need the ticket to tell me where I am going.

My, what a dust I do raise.

> ♦ Aesop's fly, sitting on the axle of a chariot

All of us invent ourselves. Some of us just have more imagination than others.

> ♦ Cher

Definition of puritanism:
The haunting fear that someone, somewhere, may be happy.

    ♦ H. L. Mencken

Smoking kills. If you're killed, you've lost a very important part of your life.

    ♦ Brooke Shields

He did not want to be taken back. What he wanted was to be recognized.

    ♦ David Malouf, "Remembering Babylon"

The "post hoc ergo propter hoc" fallacy: The rooster crows and then the sun rises, so the crowing caused the sunrise.

    ♦ Author Unknown

You don't have to piss down my back to tell me it's raining.

    ♦ Jules Miller

THIS ISN'T IT/THIS IS IT

We waste a lot of time complaining that things aren't the way we think they should be:
- *I don't have the right job.*
- *He's not the right man.*
- *I don't like the weather.*

I'm sure you've noticed how quickly things change when you complain about them. About as fast as the traffic jam disappears when you scream you don't like it, when "this isn't it" rules your life.

On the other hand, accepting life, saying "this is it," is not about giving up or rolling over without a whimper; it's more about noticing how things are, taking responsibility for your life and going on from there.

Thus play I in one person many people, and none contented. Sometimes, am I king. Then reasons make me wish myself a beggar, so I am. Then crushing penury persuades me I was better when a king. Then I am kinged again. And by and by I am unkinged, and straight, am nothing. What would ere I be, nor I, nor any man that but man is, with nothing shall be pleased, til he be eased with being nothing.

♦ William Shakespeare, "King Richard II"

Wise men in their bad hours have envied the little people making merry like grasshoppers in spots of sunlight, hardly thinking backward but never forward, and if they somehow take a hold upon the future they do it half asleep, with the tools of generation foolishly duplicating folly in thirty year periods. They eat, and laugh too, they groan against labors, wars and partings, dance, talk, dress, undress. Wise men have pretended the summer insects enviable.

♦ Robinson Jeffers

The stonecutter is the quintessential "this isn't it" guy:

THE STONECUTTER

There was once a stonecutter, who was dissatisfied with himself and with his position in life.   One day, he passed a wealthy merchant's house, and through the open gateway, saw many fine possessions and important visitors. "How powerful that merchant must be!" thought the stonecutter. He became very envious, and wished that he could be like the merchant. Then he would no longer have to live the life of a mere stonecutter.

To his great surprise, he suddenly became the merchant, enjoying more luxuries and power than he had ever dreamed of, envied and detested by those less wealthy than himself. But soon a high official passed by, carried in a sedan chair, accompanied by attendants, and escorted by soldiers beating gongs. Everyone, no matter how wealthy, had to bow low before the procession. "How powerful that official is!" he thought. "I wish that I could be a high official!"

Then he became the high official, carried everywhere in his embroidered sedan chair, feared and hated by the people all around, who had to bow down before him as he passed. It was a hot summer day, and the official felt very uncomfortable in the sticky sedan chair. He looked up at the sun. It shone proudly in the sky, unaffected by his presence. "How powerful the sun is!" he thought. "I wish I could be the sun!"

Then he became the sun, shining fiercely down on everyone, scorching the fields, cursed by the farmers and laborers. But a huge black cloud moved between him and the earth, so that his light could no longer shine on everything below. "How powerful that storm cloud is!" he thought. "I wish that I could be a cloud!"

Then he became the cloud, flooding the fields and villages, shouted at by everyone. But soon he found that he was being pushed away by some great force, and realized that it was the wind. "How powerful it is!" he thought. "I wish that I could be the wind!"

Then he became the wind, blowing tiles off the roofs of houses, uprooting trees, hated and feared by all below him. But after a while, he ran up against something that would not move, no matter how forcefully he blew against it—a huge, towering stone. "How powerful that stone is!" he thought. "I wish that I could be a stone!"

Then he became the stone, more powerful than anything else on earth. But as he stood there, he heard the sound of a hammer pounding a chisel into the solid rock, and felt himself being changed. "What could be more powerful than I, the stone?" he thought. He looked down and saw far below him the figure of a stonecutter.

♦ Author Unknown

Because I know that time is always time
And place is always and only place
And what is actual is actual only for one time
And only for one place
I rejoice that things are as they are.

♦ T.S. Eliot

There ain't any answer,
There ain't going to be any answer,
There never has been an answer,
That's the answer.

♦ Gertrude Stein

Riots and Fires and Quakes ... Oh, My!!!

♦ Kenneth Cole Billboard in Los Angeles

Before Zen study, mountains are mountains, rivers are rivers;
During Zen study, mountains are no longer mountains and rivers are no
    longer rivers;
After Zen study, mountains are mountains again and rivers are rivers.

    ♦ Zen Buddhist Saying

I gave my life to become the person I am right now. Was it worth it?

    ♦ Richard Bach, "One"

To take what there is and use it without waiting forever in vain for the preconceived—to dig deeper into the actual and get something out of that—this doubtlessly is the right way to live.

    ♦ Henry James

It was the best of times, it was the worst of times, it was the age of wisdom, it was the age of foolishness, it was the epoch of belief, it was the epoch of incredulity, it was the season of Light, it was the season of Darkness, it was the spring of hope, it was the winter of despair, we had everything before us, we had nothing before us, we are all going direct to Heaven, we were all going direct the other way.

    ♦ Charles Dickens

You want to be the person who makes it happen, and then you wonder, "What happened?"

    ♦ Mari Yamada Hollings

At the still point of the turning world. Neither flesh nor fleshless;
Neither from nor towards; at the still point, there the dance is,
But neither arrest nor movement. And do not call it fixity,
Where past and future are gathered. Neither movement from nor towards,
Neither ascent nor decline. Except for the point, the still point,

♦ T. S. Eliot

HOPE SPRINGS ETERNAL

If you care about something, hoping for it is very weak. Get serious. Make it happen. Take action.

And for those things about which you can do nothing, like the weather, you aren't helpless either.   "I hope it doesn't rain," can be followed by preparing for the possibility that it will rain.

We travel not to places but to illusions, which make every arrival both an anticlimax and a beginning.

- ♦ Mary Morris, "Nothing to Declare, Memoirs of a Woman Traveling Alone"

It is never easy to hold on to what you know
Against the undertow of what you hope to believe.

- ♦ Rebecca Hill, "Blue Rise"

People: They live for the future that will never be,
And the past that never was.

- ♦ Dan Miller

He that lives upon hope will die fasting.

- ♦ Benjamin Franklin

Harmony, like a following breeze at sea, is the exception.

- ♦ Harvey Oxenhorn, "Tuning the Rig"

What was faith? Faith was a longing that pretended to be a conviction.

   ♦ Ivan Klima, "Waiting for the Dark, Waiting for the Light"

Here's a different, quite wonderful, view of 'hope:'

Hope is an orientation of the spirit,
an orientation of the heart.
It is not the conviction that something will turn out well,
but the certainty that something makes sense,
regardless of how it turns out.

   ♦ Vaclav Havel

LANGUAGE

Words are cheap, they say. If words and actions were unrelated, then it might be true that words lack real power. But they're not. "In language," as Fernando Flores points out, "we receive the gift of being human." What we say to ourselves (called thinking) or to others (called speaking) and what we hear from ourselves and from others (called listening) has everything to do with our behavior, our actions. So words are not cheap—unless we say so.

In a large context language has majesty and can be magical. The power of language is available to each of us all the time. It is a gift that we would do well to use wisely.

We human beings belong to language. In language, we love and hate, we admire and despise. We interpret our crises as individual and social. We suffer, and exalt, and despair. In language, we receive the gift of being human. All the feeling, the thinking, the action, and the things of the world as we know it are given to us in language.

Thinking is a practice we do in life. Like all human practices, it happens in language—in a background which is normally transparent to us. To alter or open our practices to different eventualities takes exercise, discipline, and consistent observation and study. When we talk about thinking, we are concerned with opening a new future—with altering the future, and producing a future other than the future that will arrive to us out of inertia.

   ♦ Fernando Flores

Words do not label things already there. Words are like the knife of the carver. They free the idea, the thing, from the general formlessness of the outside. As a man speaks, not only is his language in a state of birth, but also the very thing about which he is talking.

   ♦ Eskimo Quote

Why, when something important happens to you, do you feel compelled to tell someone else about it? Even people who are reticent to talk about themselves can't help telling others about events significant to them. It's as if nothing has happened until an event is made explicit in language.

After much retelling, we are left with the details of the story that we have chosen to remember. Story creation is a memory process.

We need to tell someone else a story that describes our experiences because the process of creating the story also creates the memory structure that will contain the gist of the story for the rest of our lives. Talking is remembering.

♦ From "Tell Me a Story"

It is wrong to think that the task of physics is to find out how nature IS. Physics concerns what we can SAY about nature.

♦ Niels Bohr

Managers have to learn to know language, to understand what words are and what they mean. Perhaps more important, they have to acquire respect for language as our most precious gift and heritage. The manager must understand the meaning of the old definition of rhetoric as 'the art which draws men's hearts to the love of true knowledge.'

♦ Peter Drucker, "The Practice of Management"

Without context there is no communication.

♦ Gregory Bateson

THE WORD

The word that allows YES, the word that makes NO possible,

The word that put the FREE in freedom
and takes the obligation out of love,

The word that throws a window open after the final door is
closed,

The word upon which all adventure, all exhilaration,
all meaning, all honor depends,

The word that fires evolution's motor of mud,

The word that the cocoon whispers to the caterpillar,

The word that molecules recite before bonding,

The word that separates that which is dead from
that which is living,

The word no mirror can turn around.

In the beginning was the word and the word was

    CHOICE.

     ♦ Tom Robbins, "Still Life With Woodpecker"

When a man is coming toward you, you need not say: "Come here."

     ♦ African Proverb

Vaclav Havel, *then President of Czechoslovakia, reminded a Western audience in 1989 that any struggle for freedom and dignity must begin with the effort to reclaim and redeem the language, restoring true meanings to words corrupted by abusive regimes:*

At the beginning of everything is the word. It is a miracle to which we owe the fact that we are human. But at the same time it is a pitfall and a test, a snare and a trial. More so, perhaps, than it might appear to you who have enormous freedom of speech, and might therefore assume that words are not so important. They are. They are important everywhere.

The same word can be humble at one moment and arrogant the next...It is not hard to demonstrate that all the main threats confronting the world today, from atomic war and ecological disaster to a catastrophic collapse of society and civilization....have hidden deep within them a single root cause: the imperceptible transformation of what was originally a humble message into an arrogant one

Having learned from all this, we should all fight together against arrogant words and keep a weather eye out for any insidious germs of arrogance in words that are seemingly humble. Obviously this is not just a linguistic task. Responsibility for and toward words is a task which is intrinsically ethical.

Silence may speak more eloquently than words. It is the primordial attunement of one existence to another. It is only because man is capable of such silence that he is capable of authentic speech. If he ceases to be rooted in such silence it all becomes chatter.

    ♦ Martin Heidegger

True communication depends upon our being straightforward with one another.

    ♦ Shunryu Suzuki

Andrew Oerke *is an overseas development specialist and a friend who, in his spirit and heart, is a poet. Andrew's use of language is magical. His poem, "In the Village" is an expression of his long-standing love affair with Africa:*

IN THE VILLAGE

In the village in the village in the village
life repeats itself, life repeats itself.
There is sunlight; there is darkness. The dark
repeats itself, the light repeats itself;
planting repeats itself, harvest repeats
itself. Yet life is never dull. It pats
the drum-hide of the night and is satisfied.
It listens for footfalls when the dogs bark
in the village in the village in the village.

In the village in the village in the village
life repeats itself, life undoes itself
and then does itself up in the same guise.
We are careful not to fail to repeat
the same salutations, the same farewells
our parents and their parents use.
They are wise; we are small and the day long.
Death comes but once but when it comes to life
no one would be unwilling to repeat
in the village in the village in the village.

If you step on a man's foot and break a bone, it will heal. If you hurt another with your words, the wound will never heal.

◆ Sai Baba

And for a different point of view:

Sticks and stones will break my bones, but names can never hurt me.

    ◆ Childhood Saying

Humpty Dumpty: When I use a word, it means just what I choose it to mean—neither more nor less.

Alice: The question is, whether you CAN make words mean so many different things.

    ◆ Lewis Carroll, "Through the Looking Glass"

Someone was drawing water, and my teacher placed my hand under the spout. As the cool stream gushed over one hand she spelled into the other the word 'water,' first slowly, then rapidly. I stood still, my whole attention fixed upon the motions of her fingers. Suddenly I felt a misty consciousness as of something forgotten—a thrill of returning thought; and somehow the mystery of language was revealed to me.

I knew then that 'w-a-t-e-r' meant the wonderful cool something that was flowing over my hand. That living word awakened my soul, gave it light, hope, joy; set it free.

    ◆ Helen Keller, (upon realizing that everything has a 'sign' and can be communicated)

FOR SPECIAL ATTENTION:

KRISHNAMURTI

The quotes here are from a book called "Krishnamurti," *by Pupul Jayakar. Krishnamurti lived a long time—from 1895 to 1986; he was called a philosopher, an intellectual, a teacher. For me he was a thinker, pure and simple. And his thinking stimulated new thinking in others.*

When I read the book it fascinated me, and I found much to quote. Perhaps it's because his thinking is consistent with many of the themes that I focus on in this book: about the past, the future, possibilities, the unknown. He also appeals to me because he didn't try to regiment his ideas into a formalized discipline; he didn't have walls around his ideas.

On the back cover of the book is the following Krishnamurti quote:

If you follow each thought to its completion, you will see that at the end of it there is silence. From that there is renewal. Thought that arises from this silence no longer has desire as its motive force, it emerges from a state that is not clogged with memory.

But if again the thought that so arises is not completed, it leaves a residue. Then there is no renewal and the mind is caught again in a consciousness which is memory, bound by the past, by yesterday. Each thought, then to the next, is the yesterday—that which has no reality.

The new approach is to bring time to an end.

Pupul Jayakar then says: I did not understand then, but came away with the words alive within me.

She speaks for me. A lot that Krishnamurti says I don't understand, and yet his words enliven and enlighten me.

One thing he said, though, is totally understandable and incredibly powerful in its simplicity. It might be the best advice anyone will ever give you (or the best advice you could give someone):

Go and make friends with the trees.

Now, some Krishnamurti:

The Buddha, the Christ had never claimed divinity, it was the disciple who, by his worship, gave divinity to the teacher.

* * *

Two flowers or things can be similar, but not the same.

* * *

The Real is near, you do not have to seek. Truth is in 'what is,' and that is the beauty of it.

* * *

Man does not know the way, so the only thing he can do is to cease to struggle and with whatever instruments and energy he has, observe that which is the bondage. It is the simple, the sorrow-laden, the real seeker who is the hope. The simple are so crushed by their own insignificance, they do not trust the integrity of their own intentions.

* * *

Freedom from fear can only arise when man perceives the movement of fear within himself. The seeing of it is the quenching of it.

* * *

We are an old people; we wander in search for everything in far off places when it is so close to us. Beauty is ever there, never here, trust is never in our homes but in some distant place. We go to the other side of the world to find the master, and we are not aware of the servant; we do not understand the common things of life, the everyday struggles and joys and yet we attempt to grasp the mysterious and the hidden.

* * *

I am going to say 'What is' and I will follow the movement of 'What is.' Follow not my words, but the movement of thought, that is active in you. To acknowledge life 'as is,' ends conflict. The seeing of 'What is' is the freedom from 'What is.'

* * *

Understanding of the self only arises in relationship, in watching yourself in relationship to people, ideas, and things; to trees, the earth, and the world around you and within you. Relationship is the mirror in which the self is revealed. Without self-knowledge there is no basis for right thought and action.

* * *

Most of us are not aware of our relationship to nature. When we see a tree we see it with a utilitarian view—how to get to its shade, how to use its wood. Similarly, we treat the earth and its products. There is no love of the earth, only a usage of earth. If we loved the earth there would be frugality of the things of the earth. We have lost a sense of tenderness, of sensitivity. Only in the renewal of that can we understand what is relationship. That sensitivity does not come by hanging a few pictures or by putting flowers in your hair. It only comes when the utilitarian attitude is put aside. Then you no longer divide the earth, then you no longer call the earth yours or mine.

* * *

While the next four are separate, I suggest they be read as a whole thought:

Silence is there without end. I want to find out what energy is. It may be possible for it to function endlessly. But idea comes first and covers and frames silence. But silence has no end; things exist in it; they are part of it; they are not contradictory to silence. That child's crying is silence. When noise is within it, it is silence. If silence is extensive, noise is part of silence.

* * *

I can live in silence and whatever I do is not contradictory, so long as I live in silence and do not resist it. Then everything is in it except resistance. It is resistance that creates its own whirlpool, like fire the flames leap to the skies.

* * *

The moment mind as idea operates it is contradiction. But this state needs extraordinary intelligence and integrity. Since this thing is limitless, it must be energy. Here it is limitless because there is no causation. The mind creates energy that has a cause and so an end. But silence is not of the mind, and so that energy has no limit. Don't translate this to suit your mind. The mind cannot understand what is not of itself. But this is limitless. In this state everything is, but the things of the mind. In this state every noise is, and that is not noise. Then contradiction arises and mind arises and creates an exclusive pattern with its own energy.

* * *

When the little operates in the whole as part of the whole then the little is limitless. When it acts separately, then it is limited. The mind operating as part of the whole is endless.

* * *

We have cultivated intellect, which is the artificial flower. We have dug the real out from its roots. Now how is one to have love?

* * *

74

There are no answers to life's questions. The state of mind that questions is more important than the question itself. If it is a right question, it will have no answer, because the question itself will open the door. But, if it is a wrong question, you will find ways and means to solve the problem and so remain in bondage. For he who asks the question is himself the bondage.

* * *

Have you ever listened to the noise of a crow? Actually, listened to it without shutting it out as ugly. If you are capable of so listening, there is no division between the noise and what is being said. Attention implies a clarity of altogetherness, in which there is no exclusion. I have nothing to offer. If you are listening, you are already in that state. No guru is going to tell you that you are doing well. That you may go to the next examination. You are listening to yourself and that is an art.

* * *

One is everlastingly comparing oneself with another, with what one is, with what one should be, with someone who is more fortunate. This comparison really kills. Comparison is degrading, it perverts one's outlook. And on comparison one is brought up. All our education is based on it and so is our culture. So there is everlasting struggle to be something other than what one is. The understanding of what one is uncovers creativeness, but comparison breeds competitiveness, ruthlessness, ambition, which we think brings about progress. Progress has only led so far to more ruthless wars and misery than the world has ever known. To bring up children without comparison is true education.

* * *

We are not concerned with being, but with having been and becoming. There is an active present, a state of being, a living, active state. *Jayakar's note:* He spoke of listening as a state of comprehension, of being, in which all time was included.

* * *

Be supple mentally. Strength does not lie in being firm and strong but in being pliable. The pliable tree stands in a gale. *(Sounds like Chesterton)* Gather the strength of a swift mind.

* * *

The opposite of pride is not humility—it is still pride, only it is called humility; the consciousness of being humble is a form of pride.

* * *

Dignity is a very rare thing. An office or a position of respect gives dignity. It is like putting on a coat. The coat, the costume, the post gives dignity. A title or a position gives dignity. But strip man of these things, and very few have that quality of dignity that comes with inward freedom of being as nothing. Being something is what man craves for, and that something gives him a position in society which it respects. Put a man into a category of some kind—clever, rich, a saint, a physicist; but if he cannot be put into a category that society recognizes, he is an odd person. Dignity cannot be assumed, be cultivated, and to be conscious of being dignified is to be conscious of oneself, which is to be petty, small. To be nothing is to be free of that very idea. Being, not of or in a particular state, is true dignity. It cannot be taken away, it always is.

To allow the free flow of life, without any residue being left, is real awareness. The human mind is like a sieve which holds some things and lets others go. What it holds is the size of its own desires; and desires, however profound, vast, noble, are small, are petty, for desire is a thing of the mind. Not to retain, but to have the freedom of life to flow without restraint, without choice, is complete awareness. We are always choosing or holding, choosing the things that have significance and everlastingly holding on to them. This we call experience, and the multiplication of experiences we call the richness of life. The richness of life is the freedom from the accumulation of experience. The experience that remains, that is held, prevents that state in which the known is not. The known is not the treasure, but the mind clings to it and thereby destroys or defiles the unknown. Life is a strange business. Happy is the man who is nothing.

* * *

Freedom consists in having no security of any kind.

* * *

Intelligence is total freedom from fear. Those whose morality is based on security, security in every form, are not moral, for the desire for security is the outcome of fear.

* * *

Be awake, aflame.

* * *

It is only that 'which is' that can be transformed, not that which you wish to be. The understanding of what you are—ugly, beautiful, wicked, evil— understanding without distortion is the beginning of virtue. Virtue alone gives freedom.

* * *

Compassion means passion for all; love does not suffer.

* * *

Where you are the other is not.

* * *

One cannot be free if there is no sensitivity to the beauty of everything about you.

* * *

The act of learning is the act of living. Learning is a quality of mind, an attitude that is more important than what is learnt.

* * *

Two Buddhist monks came to the bank of a river and found it flooded and difficult to cross. A woman was waiting on the banks and she begged them to help her across, as her children were alone and hungry. One monk refused, the other picked her up and crossed the stream, holding her on his back. When they had crossed and were on their way again, the first monk protested vehemently. He was horrified that a monk should touch a woman, let alone carry her on his back. The second monk turned to him and said, "You mean you still carry the woman in your mind? I left her behind on the riverbank long ago."

* * *

Can you from today look at the thirty years as the past? Not from the thirty years look at today?

* * *

Ending of sorrow is the bliss of compassion.

* * *

Finally, Krishnamurti on his teachings:

The teachings were not the book. The only teachings were, 'Look at yourself. Enquire into yourself—go beyond.' There is no understanding of the teaching, only understanding of yourself. The words were a pointing of the way. The understanding of yourself the only teaching.

* * *

Question: Has there been a change in your teachings?
Answer: At the source, that river is one drop—it is the Ganga.

* * *

Look what religions have done: concentrated on the teacher and forgotten the teaching. Why do we give such importance to the person of the teacher? The teacher may be necessary to manifest the teaching, but beyond that, what? The vase contains water; you have to drink the water, not worship the vase. Humanity worships the vase, forgets the water.

* * *

MOTHER NATURE

I've never been passionate about the environment or the natural world around us. That's kind of an anomaly, because I love the mountains (at least from a distance) and the sea. And I am fascinated by wildlife and beautiful flowers, trees, etc. So I don't know why I'm not emotionally pulled to the subject. I think I'll just stay in the question and enjoy the world around me.

If we make an enemy of the earth, we make an enemy of our own body.

   ♦ Mayan Shaman

For, lo, the winter is past, the rain is over and gone; the flowers appear on the earth; the time of the singing of birds is come.

   ♦ Song of Solomon (2:11-12)

I forget exactly what Daniel Quinn was talking about, but I think it has to do with the respect, or lack of it, we show toward the world around us:

The premise of the Taker story is "the world belongs to man."
The premise of the Leaver story is "man belongs to the world."

   ♦ Daniel Quinn, "Ishmael,"

He who loves and understands nature is never afraid and never alone.

   ♦ Rachel Carson

HIT THE PAUSE BUTTON:

"DROPPING ASHES ON THE BUDDHA"
The Teaching of Zen Master Seung Sahn

Spring comes, the grass grows by itself.

* * *

The Great Way is not difficult
if you do not make distinctions.
Only throw away likes and dislikes,
and everything will be perfectly clear.

* * *

Buddha said all things have Buddha-nature.
Jo-ju said the dog has no Buddha-nature.
Which one is correct?
If you open your mouth, you fall into hell.
Why?
KATZ!!!
Clouds float up to the sky.
Rain falls down to the ground.

* * *

From Ko Bong:

The man who has come to this
is the man who was here from the beginning.
He does what he always did.
Nothing has changed.

* * *

Fish swim in the water, but they don't know they are in water. Every moment you breathe in air, but you do it unconsciously. You would be conscious of air only if you were without it.

In the same way, we are always hearing the sound of cars, waterfalls, rain. All these sounds are sermons, they are the voice of the Buddha himself preaching to us. We hear many sermons, all the time, but we are deaf to them. If we were really alive, whenever we heard, saw, smelled, tasted, touched, we would say, 'Ah, this is a fine sermon.' We would see that there is no scripture that teaches so well as this experience with nature.

* * *

Man's discriminating thoughts build up a great thought-mass in his mind, and this is what he mistakenly regards as his real self. In fact, it is a mental construction based on ignorance. The purpose of Zen meditation is to dissolve this thought-mass. What is finally left is the real self.

* * *

If you don't enter the lion's den, you will never capture the lion.

* * *

First you must find It. If you find it, you will have freedom, and no hindrance. Sometimes its name is you, sometimes me, sometimes us, sometimes earth, sometimes love, sometimes hit, sometimes the tree has no roots and the valley has no echo, sometimes three pounds of flax, sometimes dry shit on a stick, sometimes like this, and sometimes just like this.

* * *

From Kyong Ho, *upon attaining enlightenment:*

I heard about the cow with no nostrils
And suddenly the whole universe is my home.
Yon Am Mountain lies flat under the road.
A farmer, at the end of his work, is singing.

From Kyong Ho, *just before he died:*

Light from the moon of clear mind
drinks up everything in the world.
When mind and light disappear,
what...is...this...?

* * *

If you say you haven't lost it, you have already lost it. If you want to find it,
    you won't be able to find it.
All people use it all the time.
But they don't understand it, because it has no name and no form.
It pierces past, present, and future, and it fills space.
Everything is contained in it.
It is apparent in everything.
But if you want to find it, it will go further and further away,
And if you lose it, it has already appeared before you.
It is brighter than sunlight, and darker than a starless night.
Sometimes it is bigger than the universe, sometimes smaller than the point of
    a needle.
It controls everything; it is the king of the ten thousand dharmas.
It is powerful and awesome.
People call it "mind," "God," "Buddha," "nature," "energy."
But it has no beginning or end, and is neither form nor emptiness.
If you want it, then you must ride the ship which has no hull;
You must play the flute with no holes;
You must cross the ocean of life and death.
You will then arrive at the village of "like this."
Within the village, you must find your true home, "just like this."
Then, when you open the door, you will get it.
It is only "it is."

* * *

From the Mahaparinirvana Sutra:

All things are impermanent. This is the law of appearing and disappearing. When appearing and disappearing disappear, then this stillness is bliss.

* * *

Spring comes and snow melts: appearing and disappearing are just like this. The east wind blows the rain clouds west: impermanence and permanence are just like this. When you turn on the lamp, the whole room becomes bright: all truth is just like this. Form is form, emptiness is emptiness.

* * *

Go ask a child about the true way. A child will give you a good answer. Zen mind is children's mind. Children have no past or future, they are always living in the truth, which is just like this. When they are hungry, they eat; when they are tired, they rest. Children understand everything.

* * *

The Mahayana Sutra *says:*

Water becomes square or round according to the shape of the container it is put in. In the same way, people become good or bad according to the friends they have. *(See the same thought with a different conclusion in "Wisdom.")*

* * *

The blue mountains and green forests
are the Patriarchs' clear face.
Do you understand this face?
A quarter is twenty-five cents.

* * *

What is love?

One evening, after a Dharma talk at the Cambridge Zen Center, a student asked Seung Sahn Soen-sa, "What is love?"

Soen-sa said, "I ask you: what is love?"
The student was silent.
Soen-sa said, "This is love."
The student was still silent.
Soen-sa said, "You ask me: I ask you. This is love."

FACING REALITY

I think the sooner we face up to what's really in front of us the better off we are. As Jody Powell *said, "Unlike good wine, bad news does not improve with age."*

Nothing is more real than the paradigm in which we live.   What is a paradigm?   Good question:

A paradigm is a constellation of concepts, values, perceptions, and practices shared by a community (or organization), which form a particular vision of reality and a collective mood that is the basis of the way the community organizes itself.

♦ Fritjof Capra

It's not chaos that drives us crazy; it's the false expectation of order.

♦ Moral of the "Tiny the Pig" story

How strange, that when the storm is in your face, you can fight it.

♦ James Michener, "Hawaii"

Life cannot wait until the scientists have explained the universe. We cannot put off living until we are ready. The most salient characteristic of life is its coerciveness; it is always urgent, here and now without any possible postponement. Life is fired at us point blank.

♦ Jose Ortega y Gasset

Your strength is measured by how you confront your weakness.

♦ "Picket Fences" (TV Show)

A paranoid is a man who knows a little of what's going on.

    ♦ William Burroughs

"I can't give up [writing] novels."
"Why not?"
Because…because then he would be left with experience, with untranslated
and unmediated experience. Because then he would be left with life.

    ♦ Martin Amis, "The Information"

At the end of every road you meet yourself.

    ♦ S.N. Behrman

What you fix your gaze on is the little hard-backed flies that are crawling
about in the corner of its bloodshot eyes and hopping down at intervals to
drink the sweat of its lip. And the horror it carries to you is not just the
smell, in your own sweat, of a half-forgotten swamp-world going back deep
in both of you, but that for him, as you meet here face to face in the sun, you
and all you stand for have not yet appeared over the horizon of the world, so
that after a moment all the wealth of it goes dim in you, then is canceled
altogether, and you meet at last in a terrifying equality that strips the last
rags from your soul and leaves you so far out on the edge of yourself that
your fear now is that you may never get back.

    ♦ David Malouf, "Remembering Babylon" (a white man observing
       an Aboriginal Australian)

JUST BECAUSE I LIKE THEM

We shall not cease from exploration
and the end of all our exploring
will be to arrive where we started
and know the place for the first time...
A condition of complete simplicity
costing no less than everything.

And all shall be well
and all manner of things shall be well
when the tongues of flame are in-folded
into the crowned knot of fire
and the fire and the rose are one.

♦ T.S. Eliot, "Four Quartets"

How sweetly did they float upon the wings
Of silence through the empty-vaulted night,
At every fall smoothing the raven down
Of darkness till it smiled.

♦ John Milton

In Robert Bolt's play about Sir Thomas More, "A Man for All Seasons," More's son-in-law, Roper, objects when More lets an enemy go because he has violated no law. Roper says he would "cut down every law in England" to get at the Devil.

"Oh?" More says. "And when the last law was down, and the Devil turned round on you, where would you hide?"

Fill your heart with simple joy.
Traveler,
Scatter freely along the road
The treasure you gather as you go.

♦ Rabindranath Tagore, "Judgement"

Usually we hear only the beginning or ending of this poem by John Donne. *I love the whole thing:*

No man is an *Iland,* intire of it selfe;
every man is a peece of the *Continent,* a part of the *maine;*
if a *Clod* bee washed away by the *Sea, Europe* is the lesse,
as well as if a *Promontorie* were,
as well as if a *Mannor* of thy *friends* or of *thine owne* were;
any mans *death* diminishes *me,*
because I am involved in *Mankinde;*
And therefore never send to know for whom the *bell* tolls;
it tolls for *thee.*

LIFE AND DEATH/DEATH AND LIFE

Conventional wisdom tells us that facing death is the ultimate challenge. I suggest that for most of us facing life is a greater challenge. And we face it for a lot longer time.

When death comes and whispers to me
"Thy days are ended,"
let me say to him, "I have lived in love
and not in mere time."
He will ask "Will thy songs remain?"
I shall say "I know not, but this I know
that often when I sang I found my eternity."

♦ Rabindranath Tagore

My good friend, Sidney Rittenberg, *spent 16 years in solitary confinement in Chinese prison cells. The details are in his autobiography, "The Man Who Stayed Behind." About his days alone, without human contact, he says:*

I tried to assure a certain time every day of thinking quietly, of letting all the thoughts drift away, and think about what I was not thinking about, what is basic and underlying.

Among the many things Sidney has to say that are worth listening to is a philosophy of life put forward by Edwin Markham *in his poem, "Outwitted," a Sidney favorite:*

He drew a circle that shut me out,
Heretic, rebel, a thing to flout.
But love and I had the wit to win:
We drew a circle that took him in!

If the dead be truly dead, why should they still be walking in my heart?

♦ Winnenap, Shoshone Medicine Man

I could not simplify myself.

♦ Ivan Turgenev, a suicide note in "Virgin Soil"

We live, as we dream, alone.

♦ Joseph Conrad, "Heart of Darkness"

I went to the Garden of Love
And saw what I never had seen:
A chapel was built in the midst,
where I used to play on the green.

And the gates of this chapel were shut,
And 'Thou shalt not' writ over the door;
So I turned to this Garden of Love,
That so many sweet flowers bore.

And I saw it was filled with graves,
And tomb-stones where flowers should be,
And priests in black gowns were walking their rounds
and binding with briars my joys and desire.

♦ William Blake, "The Garden of Love"

The tragedy of life is not death, but what dies inside us while we live.

♦ Norman Cousins

I consider many adults (including myself) are or have been, more or less, in a hypnotic trance, induced in early infancy: we remain in this state until—when we dead awaken . . . we shall find that we have never lived.

◆ R.D. Laing, "The Politics of the Family"

Life is an experience to be lived, not a problem to be solved.

◆ Soren Kierkegaard

But let children walk with nature, let them see the beautiful blendings and communions of death and life, their joyous inseparable unity, as taught in woods and meadows, plains and mountains and streams of our blessed star, and they will learn that death is stingless indeed, and as beautiful as life, and that the grave has no victory, for it never fights.

All is divine harmony.

◆ John Muir, Naturalist

A man's dying is more his survivor's affair than his own.

◆ Thomas Mann, "A Death in Venice"

Long time to be gone,
Such a short time to be there.

◆ Grateful Dead, "Box of Rain"

You can squash a fly, but the 'thing in itself' doesn't die.

◆ Arthur Schopenhauer

Ingemar Bergman's film, "The Seventh Seal," *made a big impression on me. The Knight and Death playing a chess game, with the Knight's life at stake; outrageous actions in the name of religion. I remember in particular the flagellation scene: dozens of people marching, stumbling, crawling along as they beat themselves with sticks and whips and chains.*

One line from the film stayed with me from the moment I heard it. I never had to write it down to remember it. It is one of those personal "truths" that may be offensive to some but really speaks to me:

We make an idol of our fear and call it God.

The worst thing in life is not death.
The worst thing in life is to miss it.

    ♦ Author Unknown

This is what we fear—no sight, no sound,
No touch or taste or smell,
Nothing to think with,
Nothing to love or link with,
The anesthetic from which none come round.

    ♦ Philip Larkin, "Aubade"

The bad thing about death is not that it changes the future. It's that it leaves us alone with our memories.

    ♦ Peter Hoeg, "Smilla's Sense of Snow"

I live in fear of being alive.

    ♦ Gabriel Garcia Marquez, "Of Love and Other Demons"

To be immortal
Is commonplace, except for man.
All creatures are immortal, being
Ignorant of death.

♦ William Butler Yeats

Poor people's memory is less nourished than that of the rich; it has fewer landmarks in space because they seldom leave the place where they live, and few reference points in time throughout lives that are gray and featureless. Remembrance of things past is just for the rich. For the poor it only marks the faint traces on the path to death.

♦ Albert Camus, "The First Man"

Existence itself is the most inscrutable thing in existence.

♦ Naguib Mahfouz, "Arabian Nights and Days"

PROBLEMS

Have you ever considered how complicated things can get, what with one thing always leading to another.

♦ E.B. White

If you think the problem is bad now, just wait until you've solved it.

♦ Author Unknown

No problem is so big or so terrifying that it cannot be run away from.

♦ Charles Shulz, "Peanuts"

This situation is too serious for despair.

♦ James Madison

When the tide is out you can see all the crap on the beach.

♦ Author Unknown

The way through the world is more difficult to find than the way beyond it.

♦ Wallace Stevens, "Reply to Papini"

Adversity best discovers virtue.

♦ Francis Bacon

No problem can stand the assault of sustained thinking.

    ♦ Voltaire

There is no such thing as a problem without a gift for you in its hands. You seek problems because you need their gifts.

    ♦ Richard Bach, "Illusions"

An obstacle can call forth your best. Great coaches achieve unpredictable results by helping people break through their self-imposed limitations. They see obstacles as their opportunity for the most productive coaching.

    ♦ Tim Gallwey

A certain amount of opposition is a great help to a man. Kites rest against, not with the wind.

    ♦ John Neal

FOR SPECIAL ATTENTION:

"THE LITTLE PRINCE"
by
ANTOINE de ST. EXUPERY

I have loved "The Little Prince" for many years. It holds up over time in the face of life changing, growing older, and even when childhood innocence seems far far away. If I went back and looked again, I'm sure I'd include many more quotes. But for now, these will suffice. Do yourself a favor: read it again.

The little prince went away, to look again at the roses.

"You are not at all like my rose," he said...

"You are like my fox when I first knew him.

"He was only a fox like a hundred thousand other foxes.

"But I have made him my friend, and now he is unique in all the world."

* * *

It is such a secret place, the land of tears.

* * *

And he went back to meet the fox.

"Goodbye," he said.

"Goodbye," said the fox. "And now here is my secret, a very simple secret: It is only with the heart that one can see rightly; what is essential is invisible to the eye."

"What is essential is invisible to the eye," the little prince repeated, so that he would be sure to remember.

"It is the time you have wasted for your rose that makes your rose so important."

"It is the time I have wasted for my rose," said the little prince, so that he would be sure to remember.

"Men have forgotten this truth," said the fox. "But you must not forget it. You become responsible, forever, for what you have tamed. You are responsible for your rose..."

"I am responsible for my rose," the little prince repeated, so that he would be sure to remember.

* * *

"The men where you live," said the little prince, "raise five thousand roses in the same garden—and they do not find in it what they are looking for."

"They do not find it," I replied.

"And yet what they are looking for could be found in one single rose, or in a little water."

"Yes, that is true," I said.

And the little prince added:

"But the eyes are blind. One must look with the heart..."

HELPING OUT

It's great to be helpful. Sometimes it's even useful—but not always.

When you are confronted by any complex social system, such as an urban center or a hamster, with things about it that you're dissatisfied with and anxious to fix, you cannot just step in and set about fixing with such hope of helping...whatever you propose to do, based on common sense, will almost inevitably make matters worse rather than better.

You cannot meddle with one part of a complex system from the outside without the almost certain risk of setting off disastrous events that you hadn't counted on in other remote parts. If you want to fix something you are first obliged to understand, in detail, the whole system. Even then, the safest course seems to be to stand by and wring hands, but not to touch.

Intervening is a way of causing trouble.

If this is true, maybe some of the things that have gone wrong are the result of someone's efforts to be helpful.

    ♦ Lewis Thomas, "The Medusa and the Snail"

The tide lifts all boats

    ♦ Author Unknown

WHAT WE BELIEVE

What we believe is a two-edged sword. We can be uplifted and supported by our beliefs. We can also be severely limited by them, especially when we hold on to them in an unthinking and rigid way. What's important is to examine our beliefs from time to time so we can consciously choose, or re-choose them.

I'm not only talking about the beliefs we would call our basic values. What we believe comes into play many times every day. At work: "Here comes Sam. He's so boring." Our belief about Sam gives him no room to be different. At home: "When is he going to stop complaining about the same old thing." Our belief (preconceived assumption) pretty much assures nothing will be different.

Check it out. Notice how often your unexamined prior conclusions determine your response.

Ideas are definitely unstable, they not only can be misused, they invite misuses—and the better the idea the more volatile it is. That's because only the better ideas turn into dogma, and it is this process whereby a fresh, stimulating, humanly helpful idea is changed into robot dogma that is deadly. In terms of hazardous vectors released: the transformation of hydrogen into helium, uranium into lead, or innocence into corruption. And it is nearly as relentless.

The problem starts at the secondary level, not with the originator or developer of the idea but with the people who are attracted by it, who adopt it, who cling to it until their last nail breaks, and who invariably lack the overview, flexibility, imagination, and most importantly, sense of humor, to maintain it in the spirit in which it was hatched. Ideas are made by masters, dogma by disciples, and the Buddha is always killed on the road.

♦ Tom Robbins, "Still Life With Woodpecker"

She believed nothing and reverenced all.

♦ Edward R. Murrow (referring to a teacher who influenced him)

I don't believe in it, but it's true.

♦ Umberto Eco, "Foucault's Pendulum"

Suggestion: don't quickly dismiss this next one as anti-God:

When men stop believing in God, it isn't that they then believe in nothing; they believe in everything.

♦ G.K. Chesterton

We do not see things as they are, we see them as we are. We do not hear things as they are, we hear them as we are.

♦ The Talmud

Man is made by his belief. As he believes, so he is.

♦ Bhagavad-Gita

I can take this quote from the Gita in two ways: either it can demonstrate the limitations of a belief system or it can demonstrate the positive influence of a strong relationship with our spiritual being. So I could have included it in "The Spiritual You." But, you may have noticed, I didn't.

A great many people think they are thinking when they are merely rearranging their prejudices.

♦ William James

106

FOR SPECIAL ATTENTION:

"THE GNOSTIC GOSPELS" by ELAINE PAGELS

I really enjoyed "The Gnostic Gospels". Until recently I hadn't been much interested in books like this, but I've finally seen that the spiritual side of life is not something to ignore or reject. (See "The Spiritual You")

A long time ago I read and loved "The Last Temptation of Christ," by Nikos Kazantzakis. "The Gnostic Gospels" is not as radical as "Last Temptation," but it does appeal to my sense of irreverence and skepticism, especially about "organized religion." I can't say I've given up my opinions on the matter, but at least now I'm seriously interested and open to some new ideas.

Jesus said: If you bring forth that what is within you, what you bring forth will save you. If you do not bring forth that what is within you, what you do not bring forth will destroy you.

* * *

The Gospel of Thomas relates that when the disciples asked Jesus where they should go, he said only, "There is light within a man of light, and it lights up the whole world. If he does not shine, he is darkness." Far from legitimizing any institution, the saying directs one instead to oneself—to one's inner capacity to find one's own direction, to the "light within."

* * *

From the Gospel of Philip: God created humanity, [but now human beings] create God. That is the way it is in the world—human beings make gods, and worship their creation. It would be appropriate for the gods to worship human beings!

* * *

Jesus in the Gospel of Thomas: Recognize what is before your eyes, and what is hidden will be revealed to you.

* * *

Jesus in the Gospel of Thomas: Let him who seeks continue seeking until he finds. When he finds, he will become troubled. When he becomes troubled, he will be astonished, and he will rule over all things.

* * *

Silvanus the teacher: Knock on yourself as upon a door and walk upon yourself as on a straight road. For if you walk on the road, it is impossible for you to go astray...Open the door for yourself that you may know what is...Whatever you will open for yourself, you will open.

* * *

Jesus in the Gospel of Thomas: The Kingdom is inside of you, and it is outside of you. When you come to know yourselves, then you will be known, and you will realize that you are the sons of the living Father. But if you will not know yourselves, then you dwell in poverty, and it is you who ARE that poverty.

* * *

Jesus in Luke: The Kingdom of God is within you.

* * *

From the Book of Thomas the Contender: Whoever has not known himself has known nothing, but he who has known himself has at the same time already achieved knowledge about the depths of all things.

* * *

Religious language is a language of internal transformation; whoever perceives divine reality "becomes what he sees:"

From the Gospel of Philip: You saw the spirit, you became spirit. You saw Christ, you became Christ. You saw [the Father, you] shall become the Father...you see yourself, and what you see you shall [become].

From the Gospel of Philip: Whoever achieves GNOSIS becomes no longer a Christian, but a Christ.

* * *

Simon Magus, Hippolytus reports, claimed that each human being is a dwelling place, "and that in him dwells an infinite power...the root of the universe."

* * *

From the Gospel of Thomas: His disciples questioned him and said to him, "Do you want us to fast? How shall we pray? Shall we give alms? What diet shall we observe?" Jesus said, "Do not tell lies, and do not do what you hate."

WHAT DO YOU STAND FOR?

*This is about (drum roll) **Commitment**. The word is loaded with baggage. Zealots and purists say that without commitment you're not serious and nothing will happen. Are you committed to this relationship? Are you committed to reaching this goal? A few years ago you showed you were committed by "putting your money where your mouth is." Now you show you're committed by "walking the talk."*

When I worked in Japan I found that there is no Japanese word for "commitment." So I said it in other ways, such as "what do you really care about?" "what are you passionate about?" "what do you stand for?"

In fact, articulated or not, we're always committed to something. In addition to the nobler commitments, some people are committed to being a pain in the ass; others are committed to avoiding work; still others are committed to being right about everything; and so on.

A commitment freely chosen has great power. Saying you are committed because you think it's what you are supposed to say is a waste. So let's neither deify nor damn "commitment." What matters is the meaning and weight we give it.

Having gotten all that off my chest, I'm ready to enjoy what some people have to say about commitment.

It is all right to dedicate your life to greatness, to excellence, to humanity. It is all right for the dreams of our innocence to be occasions for action rather than cause for embarrassment.

♦ Brian Regnier

We will either find a way or make one.

♦ Hannibal

There is a distinction between involvement and commitment:
    It's like ham and eggs:
    The chicken is involved,
    But the pig is committed.

    ♦ Martina Navratilova

Once the validity of this mode of thought has been recognized, the final results appear almost simple; any intelligent undergraduate can understand them without much trouble. But the years of searching in the dark for a truth that one feels but cannot express; the intense desire and the alterations of confidence and misgiving, until one breaks through to clarity and understanding, are only known to him who has himself experienced them.

    ♦ Albert Einstein

Until one is committed there is hesitancy, the chance to draw back, always ineffectiveness.

Concerning all acts of initiative (and creation), there is one elementary truth, the ignorance of which kills countless ideas and splendid plans: that the moment one definitely commits oneself, then Providence moves too.

All sorts of things occur to help one that would never otherwise have occurred.

A whole stream of events issues from the decision, raising in one's favor all manner of unforeseen incidents and meetings and material assistance, which no man could have dreamt would have come his way.

I have learned a deep respect for one of Goethe's couplets:

"Whatever you can do, or dream you can, begin it.
Boldness has genius, power, and magic in it."

    ♦ W. H. Murray, "Scottish Himalayan Expedition"

A poet is somebody who is being and who expresses his or her being in words. This may sound easy. It isn't. A lot of people believe or think or know they are being. But that thinking or believing or knowing is not being.

Poetry is being, not knowing, or believing, or thinking. Almost anybody can learn to think or believe or know, but not a single human being can be taught to be. Why? Because when you think or you believe or you know, you are a lot of other people. But the moment you're being, you're nobody but yourself.

To be nobody but yourself in a world which is doing its best, night and day, to make you everybody else means to fight the hardest battle which any human being can fight and never stop fighting. As for expressing nobody but yourself in words, that means working just a little harder than anybody who isn't a poet can possibly imagine.

Why? Because nothing is quite as easy as using words like somebody else. We, all of us, do exactly this nearly all of the time and whenever we do it, we are not poets.

If at the end of your first ten or fifteen years of working and fighting and being, you find you've written one line of one poem, you'll be very lucky, indeed. So, my advice to all you people who wish to become poets is do something easy like learning to blow up the world. Be not only willing, but glad, to be and to work and to fight until you die.

Does this sound dismal? It isn't. It's the most wonderful life on earth, or so I feel.

♦ e. e. cummings

I would have written of me on my stone: I had a lover's quarrel with the world.

♦ Robert Frost

Commitment is what transforms a promise
into reality. It is the words that speak
boldly of your intentions. And the actions
which speak louder than the words.

It is making the time when there is none.
Coming through time after time after time,
year after year after year.

Commitment is the stuff character is made
of; the power to change the face of things.

It is daily triumph of integrity over
skepticism.

   ♦ Shearson/Lehman/American Express

Every now and then I think about my own death, and I think about my own
funeral. I don't want a long funeral. And if you get somebody to deliver the
eulogy, tell them not to talk too long. Tell them not to mention that I have a
Nobel Peace Prize. Tell them not to mention that I have three or four
hundred other awards. I'd like somebody to mention that day that Martin
Luther King, Jr. tried to give his life serving others. I'd like for somebody to
say that day that Martin Luther King, Jr. tried to love somebody.

Say that I was a drum major for justice. Say that I was a drum major for
peace. That I was a drum major for righteousness. And all of the other
shallow things will not matter. I won't have any money to leave behind. I
won't have the fine and luxurious things of life to leave behind. But I just
want to leave a committed life behind.

   ♦ Dr. Martin Luther King, Jr., February 4, 1968 (two months before
     he was killed)

To be used up is to be renewed.

   ♦ Lao Tzu

114

This is the true joy in life, the being used for a purpose recogn ... _, yourself as a mighty one; the being a force of nature instead of a feverish selfish little clod of ailments and grievances complaining that the world will not devote itself to making you happy.

I am of the opinion that my life belongs to the whole community and as long as I live it is my privilege to do for it whatever I can.

I want to be thoroughly used up when I die, for the harder I work the more I live. I rejoice in life for its own sake. Life is no "brief candle" to me. It is a sort of splendid torch which I have got hold of for the moment, and I want to make it burn as brightly as possible before handing it on to future generations.

♦ George Bernard Shaw, "Man and Superman"

The point of light in which you stand will make an infinite difference.

♦ Alexander Hamilton (In a letter to George Washington urging him to seek the Presidency)

I'm not a special person. I'm a regular person who does special things.

♦ Sarah Vaughn

If I am not for myself, who am I?
If I am not for others, what am I?
If not now, when?

♦ Rabbi Hillel

Commitment is an integrity of spirit.

♦ Karen Sandler

Wretchedness was the lot of those who hadn't the strength to be honorable nor the courage to be dishonorable. Wretchedness was the lot of those who, under all circumstances, remain in the middle.

♦ Ivan Klima, "Waiting for the Dark, Waiting for the Light"

FOR SPECIAL ATTENTION:

PAUL CHELKO

Paul Chelko is an artist/poet/philosopher. He and his wife Debbie live in Atlanta. Paul is a good friend of mine and one of the most creative people I've known. The first quote below appears on a painting Paul did. It typifies for me how whenever I am with Paul I see things I've never seen and think things I've never thought.

I seek now only that which I must lose.

  ♦ Paul Chelko

Trying always ends when I start being who I already am.

  ♦ Paul Chelko

When my sight is impeccable what was never outside of me suddenly appears.

  ♦ Author Unknown (from Paul Chelko)

Delay is the worst form of denial.

  ♦ Author Unknown (from Paul Chelko)

Trying to please someone is the highest form of silent aggression.

  ♦ Author Unknown (from Paul Chelko)

It's never a work of art until it gives up its identity as a product of man.

    ♦ Paul Chelko

Art collecting is the only socially commendable form of greed.

    ♦ Robert Hughes (from Paul Chelko)

Starvation among artists is a myth invented to ease the pain of mediocrity among the hacks.

    ♦ Paul Chelko

Taste is the enemy of art.

    ♦ Author Unknown (from Paul Chelko)

In each painting I do, there is a sweet spot that I fall in love with, become attached to. It's only when I'm willing to give up the sweet spot that I can begin to create.

    ♦ Paul Chelko

There is nothing personal about peace, it takes two of us.

    ♦ Paul Chelko

The finish is not the end; it is merely a line that is meant to be crossed.

    ♦ Author Unknown (from Paul Chelko)

Wanting to know an artist because you like his work is like wanting to know a goose because you like pate.

> ♦ Author Unknown (from Paul Chelko)

Drawing is an abbreviated language that leads one out on to the edge of madness...a no man's land, desolate and empty, where one can forge oneself newly in an identity wrought from faith.

> ♦ Paul Chelko says, "I might be the author of this quote. If not, I should have been."

If you're not living on the edge you're taking up too much space.

> ♦ Author Unknown (from Paul Chelko)

And time is a gentle gift.

> ♦ From a Paul Chelko Painting

HIT THE PAUSE BUTTON:

FORREST GUMP

Some wisdom from Forrest Gump:

- Never wear a belt and suspenders at the same time: people might think you are paranoid.

- Beware of people that put numbers after their names.

- Life can be one big toilet, so for all of our sakes, don't make waves.

- Most people don't look dumb till they start talkin'.

- Do not suck your thumb—or anyone else's for that matter.

- Don't ever pick a fight with somebody that's really ugly lookin'.

- Remember this: while somebody is down there kissin' your butt, they could just as easily be bitin' it, too.

- If you want to be popular, do not engage in child molestin' or line dancin'.

- Don't lick nothin' that's gonna stick to your tongue.

- Some people, like me, are born idiots, but many more become stupider as they go along.

TRUST YOURSELF

There is this thing called intuition, or instinct. It's the thought that flits across my consciousness saying I should check this or that out, maybe all isn't as I assume it to be. Too often, when I don't pay attention to that thought, I am sorry later.

It also occurs for me as a nagging question. A discussion is underway; everything seems together and logical, and yet I have nagging sense that we are missing something. I have learned to raise the question, even if I don't know what's wrong or even that anything is wrong. In the inquiry that follows either I will see what was nagging at me and be able to articulate it, or I will resolve the matter and am no longer troubled.

The moral: Trust yourself.

What I like about experience is that it is such an honest thing. You may take any number of wrong turnings; but keep your eyes open and you will not be allowed to go very far before the warning signs appear. You may have deceived yourself, but experience is not trying to deceive you. The universe rings true wherever you fairly test it.

    ♦ C.S. Lewis

There is too little recognition of the vast difference between the world as described and the world as sensed.

    ♦ Alan Watts

JUST BECAUSE I LIKE IT:

SISYPHUS

In November 1986, I attended a Symposium led by Werner Erhard. In it he talked about the "Myth of Sisyphus" and "The Bound Man." The first part is a quote from something Camus wrote about the Sisyphus myth. I'm not sure who wrote the part about "The Bound Man."

I am tempted to put my own interpretation on these pieces, but I'd rather you give them your own.

The Gods had condemned Sisyphus to ceaselessly rolling a rock to the top of a mountain, whence the stone would fall back of its own weight. They had thought with some reason that there is no more dreadful punishment than futile and hopeless labor...

Sisyphus is the absurd hero, as much through his passions as through his torture. His scorn of the gods, his hatred of death, and his passion for life won him that unspeakable penalty in which the whole being is exerted toward accomplishing nothing. This is the price that must be paid for the passions of this earth...

One sees the whole effort of a body straining to raise the huge stone, to roll it and push it up a slope a hundred times over. One sees the face screwed up, the cheek tight against the stone, the shoulder bracing the clay-covered mass, the foot wedging it, the fresh start with arms outstretched, the wholly human security of two earth-clotted hands.

At the very end of his long effort measured by skyless space and time without depth, the purpose is achieved. Then Sisyphus watches the stone rush down in a few moments toward that lower world when he will have to push it up again toward the summit. He goes back down to the plain.

It is during that return, that pause, that Sisyphus interests me. A face that toils so close to stones is already stone itself. I see that man going back

125

down with a heavy yet measured step toward the torment of which he will never know the end.

That hour, like a breathing space which returns as surely as his suffering, that is the hour of consciousness. At each of those moments when he leaves the heights and gradually sinks towards the lairs of the gods, he is superior to his fate. He is stronger than his rock.

If this myth is tragic, that is because its hero is conscious... Sisyphus, powerless and rebellious, knows the whole extent of his wretched condition. It is what he thinks of during his descent. The lucidity that was to constitute his torture at the same time crowns his victory...

Crushing truths perish from being acknowledged.   Thus, Sophocles' Oedipus, blind and desperate, says, "Despite so many ordeals, my advanced age and the nobility of my soul make me conclude that all is well."..."I conclude that all is well," says Oedipus, and that remark is sacred. It echoes in the wild and limited universe of man. It teaches that all is not, has not been, exhausted...

It makes of fate a human matter, which must be settled among men. All Sisyphus' silent joy is contained therein. His fate belongs to him. His rock is his thing...

I leave Sisyphus at the foot of the mountain. One always finds one's burden again. But Sisyphus teaches the higher fidelity that negates the gods and raises rocks. He too concludes that all is well... The struggle itself toward the heights is enough to fill a man's heart. One must imagine Sisyphus happy.

That's what Camus has to say. Now, "The Bound Man:"

The premise [of "The Bound Man"] is that the greatest achievements can be achieved through self-imposed limitations.

The bound man... is in much the same situation as Sisyphus. His freedom removed, his will frustrated, his energies devoted to a cause that is absurd.

126

And yet, like Sisyphus, he finds some element of freedom within his restrictions...

The bound man awakens one morning to find himself bound from head to toes.

Erhard: He wakes up to his own humanity, to his own pettiness, to his own limitations, to his own desires that will never be realized. He wakes up to the human condition.

Like a Kafka antagonist, he accepts his fate. His limitations have been imposed by some cosmic force he does not even try to understand. He is bound. That is the fact of his existence, and he must confront the new situation with cunning and skill.

He adapts. He makes himself a free man by working within the restrictions of his bounds. He gains his maximum freedom whenever he finds himself in harmony with the ropes, which, rather than limiting him, afford him a kind of liberty which he has never before enjoyed.

A further freedom that the bound man enjoys is the knowledge that at any time he can slip off the ropes. He has, as it were, an advantage over the man who suffers no restrictions. He can, in effect, lead a double life of intense awareness.

Of course, if he unties himself, he is like everyone else. He loses his sole mark of identity. Therefore, his reluctance to undo the ropes even when sleeping is obvious. It is sufficient for him to have the knowledge of his potential freedom from the ropes. The actual fact is unimportant.

FOR SPECIAL ATTENTION:

BUCKY FULLER

If anyone deserves special attention it's this man. Buckminster Fuller has to have been one of the most creative people who ever lived. His ideas stretch our credulity and our reality. To be in the presence of his ideas—whether you agree with them or not—is a transforming experience. Here are just a few:

Whenever I draw a circle
Immediately I want to jump out of it.

* * *

Man is born with legs and not roots. His principle advantage as a species is mobility.

* * *

I live on earth at present and I don't know what I am.
I know that I am not a category.
I am not a thing—a noun.
I seem to be a verb.

* * *

Never design something you can already build.

* * *

Our beds are empty 2/3 of the time
Our living rooms are empty 7/8 of the time
Our offices buildings are empty 1/2 of the time
It's time we gave this some thought.

* * *

...may think I'm taking up a lot of your time, but I don't think that man has much time

* * *

The only thing about me is that I am an average, healthy human being. All the things I've been able to do, any human being, or anyone, or you, could do equally well or better. I was able to accomplish what I did by refusing to be hooked on a game of life that had nothing to do with the way the universe was going. I was just a throwaway who was willing to commit myself to what needed to be done.

* * *

You can't change people—but you can change the environment and people will change.

SACRED COWS

With all due respect to my Hindu friends, I love to gore sacred cows, particularly those that are held with great reverence and certainty by sanctimonious, righteous assholes. (I wonder if I have any energy on this?) So bring them on.

A great deal of what we call 'discussion' is not deeply serious, in the sense that there are all sorts of things which are held to be non-negotiable and not touchable, and people don't even want to talk about them. This is part of our trouble.

♦ David Bohm

Symbols are very important—as long as they are grounded in values.

♦ Mary Robinson, President of Ireland

There would never have been an infidel if there hadn't been a priest.

♦ Thomas Jefferson

COMMUNITY

The quote that got me started on this section caught my eye because I lived in the Boerum Hill section of Brooklyn for almost ten years. With gentrification, public housing and an influx of Hispanic people, Boerum Hill didn't remind me of the old style neighborhoods to which Hershon refers. In the Boerum Hill of today I don't think the butcher would come to the funeral.

But there were other neighborhoods in Brooklyn that would have qualified, especially the remaining Italian ones, and so I can relate to the feeling here. It is something special. And it is something that is going away. Too bad.

boerum hill?
it used to be
gowanus
this ain't no
neighborhood
if ya butcher
comes to ya funeral
that's a
neighborhood

♦ Robert Hershon

All real living is meeting.

♦ Martin Buber

You alone can do it, but you can't do it alone.

♦ Michael Jordan

We are discovering that the physical world is not built of independently existing unanalyzable entities, but rather that all that exists is a web of relationships.

♦ A Study of Quantum Mechanics

And let's not forget our global community:

And I strive to discover
    how to signal my companions...
To say in time a simple word,
    a password, like conspirators:
Let us unite,
Let us hold each other tightly,
Let us merge our hearts,
Let us create for Earth a brain and a heart,
Let us give a human meaning to the superhuman struggle.

♦ Nikos Kazantzakis

WHAT ARE THE ODDS?

The race is not always to the swift,
nor the battle to the strong,
but that's the way to bet.

♦ Damon Runyon

Yeah, the lion and the lamb shall lie down together, but the lamb won't get much sleep.

♦ Woody Allen

The less you bet, the more you lose when you win.

♦ Flip Wilson

Play for more than you can afford to lose and you learn to play the game.

♦ Winston Churchill

I think Flip and Winnie have been talking to each other.

Top accomplishment happens when we care a lot and still have fun. Far from being a function of frivolity, 'grand fun' has to do with guts, complete commitment, and a kind of fatal preference for the slim chance.

♦ Sidney Fox

You can run faster with 100 people running with you
Than with one person hanging around your neck.

♦ Les Brown

SENIOR CITIZENS

*I can't say I relate well to old people. I mean **really** old, i.e., a lot older than I am. I don't know why this is. I think it isn't a polite thing to say or think, but it's true for me. It's like me and children. I don't like kids. They're self-absorbed pains in the ass, and noisy too. (My daughter was an exception of course.)*

I held this feeling about kids as a secret for most of my life. Then, one day I heard a woman say, "I really don't like kids." I thought, "Wow, she's speaking for me." And so I admitted it, to myself and others. Telling the truth about this was very freeing.

About old people, I'm uncomfortable around their decline. It's depressing. I'd rather look the other way.

Maybe I'm talking about old people who lack energy and an ability to live life fully and cheerfully. As I think about it I really enjoy healthy older people. I think they have great faces and great wisdom. Now I can see that my issue is with sickness and feebleness, not with old people. This is a useful insight for me.

The greatest good fortune for the old person, even greater than health, is to have his world still inhabited by projects; then, busy and useful, he escapes from boredom and from decay.

♦ Simone de Beauvoir

The man who works and is never bored, is never old. A person is not old until regrets take the place of hopes and plans.

♦ Scott Nearing

There is nothing more beautiful in this world than a healthy, wise old man.

♦ Lin Yutang

When the Elders stop singing the old songs and there are no more dreams or visions of greatness, there is no more power.

So as your vision is, so shall your strength be.

So as your faith is, so shall your success be.

♦ Phil Lane, Jr., Yankton Sioux & Chickasaw Indian

A human being would certainly not grow to be 70 or 80 years old if this longevity had no meaning for the species. The afternoon of human life must also have a significance of its own, and cannot be merely a pitiful appendage to life's morning.

♦ C.G. Jung

Old men ought to be explorers
Here and there does not matter
We must be still and still moving
into another intensity
For a further union, a deeper communion
through the dark cold and the empty desolation.
The wave cry, the wind cry, the vast waters
Of the petrel and the porpoise. In my end
is my beginning.

♦ T.S. Eliot, "East Coker, Four Quartets"

Money won't change you, but time will take you on.

♦ James Brown

The view after 70 is breathtaking. What is lacking is someone, anyone, of the older generation to whom you can turn when you want to satisfy your curiosity about some detail of the landscape of the past. There is no longer any older generation. You have become it, while your mind was mostly on other matters.

♦ William Maxwell

HIT THE PAUSE BUTTON:

"THE DANCING WU LI MASTERS"

I read "The Dancing Wu Li Masters" *a long time ago. I know I liked it; I know I extracted a number of quotes from it; and now I can't even find it to remind me who wrote it, etc. I'll probably run across it some day, but in the meantime, this is what I've got.*

Based on these quotes, the sub-text here is "what's really real?" I love the question because it challenges our smugness about things. It especially challenges those of us who think we "know" something. (See "I Already Know That.") I don't know anything about quantum mechanics, or particle theory, or subatomic matter; I accept the scientific validity of the assertions made here. What's important to me is that the scientific conclusions support my non-scientific ideas, and that's the game isn't it, getting support for my opinions?

In our endeavor to understand reality we are somewhat like a man trying to understand the mechanism of a closed watch.

He will never be able to compare his picture with the real mechanism and he cannot even imagine the possibility of the meaning of such a comparison.

♦ Albert Einstein

* * *

Not one person alive has ever seen a hydrogen atom.

* * *

At the subatomic level, we cannot observe something without changing it.

* * *

e mind can ponder is its ideas about reality. Whether or not something is true is not a matter of how closely it corresponds to the absolute truth, but of how consistent it is with our experience.

* * *

According to quantum mechanics there is no such thing as objectivity.

Quantum mechanics views subatomic particles as "tendencies to exist" or "tendencies to happen," expressed in terms of probabilities.

* * *

Light behaves like waves or like particles depending upon which experiment we perform. The "we" that does the experimenting is the common link that connects light as particles and light as waves.

* * *

We are so used to the idea that an atom is a thing that we forget that it is an idea. Now we are told that not only is an atom an idea, it is an idea that we cannot even picture.

* * *

Nonsense is nonsense only when we have not yet found that point of view from which it makes sense.

Scientists are those who do not fear to venture boldly into nonsense.

* * *

The search for the ultimate stuff of the universe ends with the discovery that there isn't any.

* * *

"Knowledge," wrote e.e. cummings, "is a polite word for dead, but not buried, imagination."

* * *

The creative has two characteristics. The first is a childlike ability to see the world as it is, and not as it appears according to what we know about it.

A Zen story: Nanin poured his visitor's cup full, and then kept on pouring. Tea was everywhere. "Stop," his visitor said, "it is overfull. No more will go in!" "Like this cup," Nanin said, "you are full of your own opinions and speculations. How can I show you Zen unless you first empty your cup?"

Our cup usually is filled to the brim with "the obvious," "common sense," and the "self evident."

In the Beginner's Mind there are many possibilities, but in the expert's there are few.

The second characteristic of true artists and true scientists is the firm confidence which both of them have in themselves.

* * *

Subatomic particles are not made of energy, they are energy.

* * *

The history of scientific thought, if it teaches us anything at all, teaches us the folly of clutching ideas too closely.

* * *

The special theory of relativity also tells us that space and time are not two separate things, but that together they form spacetime, and that energy and mass are actually different forms of the same thing, massenergy.

If I am sitting in a chair and another person walks past me, then the person walking past me is in motion, and I, sitting in my chair, am not in motion.

"Quite right," says Jim de Wit, appearing on cue, "but still, it is not that simple. Suppose that the chair in which you are sitting is on an airplane and that the person walking past you is a stewardess. Suppose also that I am on the ground watching both of you go by. From your point of view, you are at rest and the stewardess is in motion, but from my point of view, I am at rest and both of you are in motion. It all depends upon your frame of reference. Your frame of reference is the airplane, but my frame of reference is the earth."

The earth itself hardly is standing still.

If we start playing that game, it is impossible to find anything in the entire universe that is "standing still."

* * *

Everything a particle physicist knows about subatomic particles, he deduces from his theories and from photographs of the tracks that particles leave in a bubble chamber.

* * *

Quantum mechanics tells us the same thing that Tantric Buddhists have been saying for a millenium. The connection between the dots (the "moving object") is a product of our minds and it is not really there. The particle is an unprovable assumption.

* * *

Our culture has taught us to perceive only the explicate order (the Cartesian view). "Things" to us are intrinsically separate.

Bohm's physics require, in his words, a new "instrument of thought."

We are reorienting it toward a perception of the "unbroken wholeness" of which everything is a form.

* * *

Any answer is only a point of view. A point of view itself is limiting. To "understand" something is to give up some other way of conceiving it.

* * *

Reality is what we take to be true. What we take to be true is what we believe. What we believe is based upon our perceptions. What we perceive depends upon what we look for. What we look for depends upon what we think. What we think depends upon what we perceive. What we perceive determines what we believe. What we believe determines what we take to be true. What we take to be true is our reality. *(See "Whatever Goes Around Comes Around")*

I GIVE UP

We're so skilled at being resigned we don't even notice we're resigned. If I were cynical I'd say it's the default position for most of life for most people. But I'm not cynical, so I won't say that.

If you think about it, giving up is a great way to have boredom be acceptable, because when you're resigned you're also bored—and boring.

And if you think about it some more, you'll see that when giving up is OK with you it infiltrates every aspect of your life.

What forces us to lie is frequently the feeling that it's impossible that others could comprehend our actions entirely.

♦ Paul Valery

We live in the gap between our resignation and our expectations
Rather than the gap between our current reality and our vision.

♦ Eric Helt

If it's true that you learn from adversity, then I must be the smartest SOB in the world.

♦ Gene Mauch, Baseball Manager

A thing of beauty is a joy till sunrise.

♦ Arnold, Female Impersonator in "Torch Song Trilogy"

MASTERY

I'm annoyed I don't have more quotes about Mastery. I know that regarding Mastery there are many thoughts, suggestions, paths, self-styled experts and maybe even a few Masters to listen to. Don't know why I didn't find more. Drat!!

It resists definition, yet it can be instantly recognized. It comes in many variations, yet follows certain unchanging laws. It makes us, in the words of the Olympic motto, "softer, higher, stronger," yet is not really a goal or a destination, but rather a process, or journey.

We call this journey mastery and tend to assume that it requires a special ticket available only to those born with exceptional abilities. But mastery is not reserved for the super-talented, or even for those who are fortunate enough to have gotten an early start. It is available to anyone who is willing to get on the path and stay on it—regardless of age, sex, or experience.

The problem is that we have few, if any, maps to guide us on the journey, or even to show us how to find the path. The modern world can be viewed as a prodigious conspiracy against mastery. We are bombarded with promises of fast, temporary relief; immediate gratification; and instant success, all of which lead in exactly the wrong direction.

◆ George Leonard, "Mastery: The Secret of Ultimate Fitness"

What the caterpillar calls the end of the world, the master calls a butterfly.

◆ Richard Bach

We seek not to imitate the masters, rather we seek what they sought.

◆ Eastern Philosophy

He, reading books, waded through tens of thousands of scrolls. When he put his pen to paper it was as if a God was writing.

- An 85-year-old Chinese poet/calligrapher (from a scroll in my home)

THE FUTURE ISN'T FAR AWAY

This is the flip side of "The Past Lives On." Here we can see we're not helpless, even though the past has a firm grip on us.

Life can only be understood backwards, but it must be lived forwards.

 ♦ Soren Kierkegaard

"Ah yes," Merlin said, "How did I know to set breakfast for two? Now ordinary people are born forwards in time, if you understand what I mean, and nearly everything in the world goes forward too. This makes it quite easy for ordinary people to live. But unfortunately I was born at the wrong end of time, and I have to live backwards from in front, while surrounded by a lot of people living forward from behind."

 ♦ T.H. White, "The Once and Future King"

It seems that the mind, working in pictures, knows no difference between a picture from the past and a picture from the future. If you create a vision as a memory in the future it will have the same power as a memory of the past.

 ♦ Harvey Austin

"I want to fly like that," Jonathan said, and a strange light glowed in his eyes. "Tell me what to do."

Chiang spoke slowly and watched the younger gull ever so carefully...

"To fly as fast as thought, to anywhere that is," he said, "you must begin by knowing that you have already arrived."

 ♦ Richard Bach, "Jonathan Livingstone Seagull"

ugh the day were here.

♦ Friedrich Nietzsche

Thanks for the future you left behind.

♦ Craig Trojahn

When we endeavor to develop ourselves in the present, we will grow toward our future goals until they are accomplished. The present naturally leads us to the future, and the future changes according to how we live in the present.

♦ Tartnang Tulku

The best way to predict the future is to invent it.

♦ John Sculley

The future belongs to those who believe the beauty of their dreams.

♦ Eleanor Roosevelt

No one can foresee the future, not even those who make it.

♦ Anatole France

There is no path. The path is made by walking.

♦ Japanese Proverb

The future is not someplace we're going to, but one we are creating. The paths are not to be found, but made, and the activity of making them changes both the maker and the destination.

♦ Professor John Schaar

The first thing you have to learn about history is that because something has not taken place in the past, that does not mean it cannot take place in the future.

♦ Mahatma Gandhi

After the final no
There comes a yes
And on that yes
The future of the world depends.

♦ Wallace Stevens

By what men think, we create the world around us, daily new.

♦ King Arthur's Sister

THE TRUTH

I was once told: "The truth shall set you free, but until it does it'll piss you off." Maybe.

Mahatma Gandhi noted that in his language the word for untruth meant "nonexistent" and the word for truth meant "that which is."

He declared, "If untruth does not so much as exist, its victory is out of the question."

As for truth, being "that which is," it can "never be destroyed."

♦ Author Unknown

Se non e vero, e ben trovato—If it's not true, it might as well be.

♦ Italian Saying

Just because someone lies about something doesn't mean it isn't true.

♦ Author Unknown

Those who know the truth are not equal to those who love it.

♦ Confucius

My aim is to teach you to pass from a piece of disguised nonsense to something that is patent nonsense.

♦ Ludwig Wittgenstein

Transparent Man, who is seen and seen through, foolish, who has nothing left to hide, who has become transparent through self-acceptance; his soul is loved, wholly revealed, wholly existential; his is just what he is, freed from paranoid concealment, from the knowledge of his secrets and his secret knowledge; his transparency serves as a prism for the world and the not-world. For it is impossible reflectively to know thyself; only the last reflection of an obituary may tell the truth, and only God knows our real names.

♦ James Hillman, "Myth of Analysis"

The truth that makes men free is for the most part the truth which men prefer not to hear.

♦ H. Agar, "A Time for Greatness"

seeker of truth

follow no path
all paths lead where

truth is here

♦ e.e. cummings

It is an indication of truth's jealousy that it has not made for anyone a path to it, and that it has not deprived anyone of the hope of attaining it, and it has left people running in the deserts of perplexity and rowing in the seas of doubt; and he who thinks that he has attained it, it dissociates itself from, and he who thinks that he has dissociated himself from it has lost his way. Thus there is no attaining it and no avoiding it—it is inescapable.

♦ Naguib Mahfouz, "Arabian Nights and Days"

The passion for truth is silenced by answers which have t'
undisputed authority.

♦ Paul Tillich

There are many ways to interpret this next one. It's from a song written and sung by Ben Harper, *a unique and special talent. I asked Sandra Marsh, the woman I share my life with, for her opinion, because while I loved the quote I couldn't settle on an interpretation. She said something that clicked. In her view it refers to insincerity from people who should be straight with you; sugar-coated communication rather than the truth. As always, you decide for yourself:*

The stones from my enemies
These wounds will mend,
But I cannot survive
The roses from my friends.

JUST BECAUSE I LIKE THEM

The eye of desire dirties and distorts. Only when we desire nothing, only when our gaze becomes pure contemplation, does the soul of things (which is beauty) open itself to us. If I inspect a forest with the intention of buying it, renting it, cutting it down, going hunting in it, or mortgaging it, then I do not see the forest but only its relation to my desires, plans, and concerns, to my purse. Then it consists of wood, it is young or old, healthy or diseased. But if I want nothing from it but to gaze, "thoughtlessly," into its green depths, then it becomes a forest, nature, a growing thing; only then is it beautiful. *(Notice the Krishnamurti in this?)*

So it is with people, and with people's faces too. The man whom I look at with dread or hope, with greed, designs, or demands, is not a man but a cloudy mirror of my own desire. Whether I am aware of it or not, I regard him in the light of questions that limit and falsify: Is he approachable, or arrogant? Does he respect me? Is he a good prospect for a loan? Does he understand anything about art?

A thousand such questions are in our minds as we look at most people we have to deal with, and we are considered expert psychologists if we succeed in detecting in their appearance, manner and behavior whatever it is that will abet or hinder our plans. But this attitude is a shabby one, and in this kind of psychology the peasant, the peddler, the shyster lawyer are superior to most politicians and scholars.

At the moment when desire ceases and contemplation, pure seeing, and self surrender begin, everything changes. Man ceases to be useful or dangerous, interesting or boring, genial or rude, strong or weak. He becomes nature, he becomes beautiful and remarkable as does everything that is an object of clear contemplation. For indeed contemplation is not scrutiny or criticism, it is nothing but love. It is the highest and most desirable state of our souls: undemanding love.

♦ Herman Hesse, "Concerning the Soul"

159

Know your enemy as you know yourself and you need not fear a hundred battles; know yourself but not the enemy, for every victory gained you will also suffer a defeat; know neither the enemy nor yourself and you will succumb in every battle.

♦ Sun-tzu

The choice was simple: To kill or not to kill, or listen or not to listen. When he was very young his mother had said, "Beware, my son, and remember seriously: to kill is easy, to unkill impossible."

♦ James Clavell, "Gaijin"

Salman Rushdie *is an amazing writer.* *These are from* "The Moor's Last Sigh:"

In the end, stories are what's left of us, we are no more than the few tales that persist.

* * *

The parable of the scorpion and the frog: The scorpion, having hitched a ride across a stretch of water in return for a promise not to attack his mount, breaks his vow and administers a potent and fatal sting. As the frog and scorpion are both drowning, the murderer apologizes to his victim. "I couldn't help it," says the scorpion. "It's in my nature."

* * *

There is a fashion nowadays for these Hitler's-valet type memoirs, and many people are against them. They say we should not humanize the inhuman. But the point is they are not inhuman, these little Hitlers, and it is in their humanity that we must locate our collective guilt, humanity's guilt for human beings' misdeeds; for if they are just monsters—if it is just a question of King Kong and Godzilla wreaking havoc until the airplanes bring them down—then the rest of us are excused.

HIT THE PAUSE BUTTON:

EXPERTS ON WHAT'S POSSIBLE

Listen to the experts speak:

Everything that can be invented has been invented.

    ♦ Charles H. Duell, Director, U.S. Patent Office, 1899

Who the hell wants to hear actors talk?

    ♦ Harry M. Warner, Warner Bros. Pictures, 1927

Sensible and responsible women do not want to vote.

    ♦ Grover Cleveland, 1905

There is no likelihood man can ever tap the power of the atom.

    ♦ Robert Millikan, Nobel Prize in Physics, 1923

Heavier than air flying machines are impossible.

    ♦ Lord Kelvin, President, Royal Society, 1835

Babe Ruth made a mistake when he gave up pitching.

    ♦ Tris Speaker, 1921

What will the soldiers and sailors, what will the common people say to 'George Washington, President of the United States?' They will despise him to all eternity.

- ♦ John Adams, 1789

Man will never reach the moon regardless of all future scientific advances.

- ♦ Lee DeForest (inventor of the audion tube), 1957

Among the really difficult problems of the world, the Arab-Israeli conflict is one of the simplest and most manageable.

- ♦ Walter Lippmann, 1948

The energy produced by the breaking down of the atom is a very poor kind of thing. Anyone who expects a source of power from the transformation of the atom is talking moonshine.

- ♦ Lord Rutherford, Nobel Laureate, 1933

You ain't goin' nowhere...son. You ought to go back to driving a truck.

- ♦ Jim Denny, Grand Ole Opry manager, firing Elvis Presley after one performance, 1954

There is no reason for any individual to have a computer in their home.

- ♦ Ken Olsen, President of Digital Equipment, 1977

I DECLARE

I love declarations. They're different than other kinds of statements, because they really can't be held to objective proof. The answer to "prove it" is "I said so."

"We declare these truths to be self evident, that all men are created equal." Our Declaration of Independence didn't make all men equal; it didn't tell us how to make sure that all men are created equal. It opened up the door, declared the possibility, that all men are created equal.

A declaration is very much like a commitment, which I talk about in "What Do You Stand For." If our stand is that all men are created equal, and we're serious about it, then what we do, the actions we will take, will forward that possibility.

Declarations come in many forms. Umpires, calling balls and strikes at a baseball game, are making declarations:

The rookie umpire will say: I calls 'em like I sees 'em.

The journeyman umpire will say: I call 'em like they are.

The master umpire will say: They ain't nothin' 'til I call 'em.

♦ Author Unknown

Der ain't no close plays, me lad. Dey is either dis or dat.

♦ Bill Guthrie, Umpire

How we choose to live our lives can also be a declaration:

All it takes to make a difference is the courage to stop proving I was right in being unable to make a difference, to stop assigning the cause for my inability to the circumstances outside myself, and to see that the fear of being a failure is a lot less important than the unique opportunity I have to make a difference.

    ♦ Werner Erhard

What we truly and earnestly declare ourselves to be, that in some sense we are. The mere declaration, by changing the frame of the mind, for the moment realizes itself.

    ♦ Anna Jameson

FOR SPECIAL ATTENTION:

JOSEPH CAMPBELL

Bill Moyers' *PBS series on and with* Joseph Campbell *inspired me to go out and buy Campbell's book, "The Power of Myth." What follows are quotes from various parts of the book, much of which is a dialogue between Campbell and Moyers.*

From the Introduction by Moyers:

[About] having me as a pupil, [Campbell] quoted an old Roman: "The fates lead him who will; him who won't they drag."

Comparable stories [Campbell said] can be found in divergent traditions—stories of creation, of virgin births, incarnations, death and resurrection, second comings, and judgment days. He liked the insight of the Hindu scripture: "Truth is one; the sages call it by many names."

[Campbell] was a man with a thousand stories: A social philosopher from New York says to a Shinto priest, "We've been now to a good many ceremonies and have seen quite a few of your shrines. But I don't get your ideology. I don't get your theology." The Japanese paused as though in deep thought and then slowly shook his head. "I think we don't have ideology," he said. "We don't have theology. We dance."

* * *

Campbell: There's no meaning. What's the meaning of the universe? What the meaning of a flea? It's just there. That's it. And your own meaning is that you're there. We're so engaged in doing things to achieve purposes of outer value that we forget that the inner value, the rapture that is associated with being alive, is what it's all about.

Campbell: If you want to find out what it means to have a society without any rituals, read the New York Times. The news of the day includes many destructive and violent acts by young people who don't know how to behave in a civilized society.

Moyers: Society has provided them no rituals by which they become members of the tribe, of the community.

Campbell: That's the significance of the puberty rites.

Moyers: Where do these kids get their myths today?

Campbell: They make them up themselves. This is why we have graffiti all over the city. These kids have their own gangs and their own initiations and their own morality, and they're doing the best they can. But they're dangerous because their own laws are not those of the city. They have not been initiated into our society.

* * *

Cambell: Now, eternity is beyond all categories of thought. This is an important point in all of the great Oriental religions. We want to think about God. God is a thought. God is a name. God is an idea. But its reference is to something that transcends all thinking. The ultimate mystery of being is beyond all categories of thought.

As Kant said, the thing in itself is no thing. It transcends thingness, it goes past anything that could be thought. The best things can't be told because they transcend thought. The second best are misunderstood, because those are the thoughts that are supposed to refer to that which can't be thought about. The third best are what we talk about. And myth is that field of reference to what is absolutely transcendent.

* * *

Campbell: The central point of the world is the point where stillness and movement are together. Movement is time, but stillness is eternity.

* * *

Moyers: We talked about the effect of the hunting plain on mythology, this space clearly bounded by a circular horizon with the great dome of heaven above. But what about the people who lived in the dense foliage of the jungle? There's no dome of the sky, no horizon, no sense of perspective—just trees, trees, trees.

Campbell: Colin Turnbull tells an interesting story of bringing a pygmy who had never been out of the forest onto a mountaintop. Suddenly they came from the trees onto the hill, and there was an extensive plain stretching out before them. The poor little fellow was utterly terrified. He had no way of judging perspective or distance. He thought that the animals grazing on the plain in the distance were just across the way and were so small that they were ants. He was just totally baffled, and rushed back into the forest.

* * *

Campbell: Just sheer life cannot be said to have a purpose, because look at all the different purposes it has all over the place. But each incarnation, you might say, has a potentiality, and the mission of life is to live that potentiality. How do you do it?

My answer is, "Follow your bliss." There's something inside you that knows when you're in the center, that knows when you're on the beam or off the beam.

Moyers: Do you ever have this sense when you are following your bliss, as I have at moments, of being helped by hidden hands?

Campbell: All the time. It is miraculous. I even have a superstition that has grown on me as the result of invisible hands coming all the time—namely, that if you do follow your bliss you put yourself on a kind of track that has been there all the while, waiting for you, and the life that you ought to be living is the one you are living. When you can see that, you begin to meet people who are in the field of your bliss, and they open the doors to you. I say, follow your bliss and don't be afraid, and doors will open where you didn't know they were going to be.

Moyers: Have you ever had sympathy for the man who has no invisible means of support?

Campbell: Yes, he is the one that evokes compassion, the poor chap.

* * *

Campbell: If you are following you bliss, you are enjoying that refreshment, that life within you, all the time.

* * *

Campbell: Love thine enemies because they are the instruments of your destiny.

* * *

Campbell: Karlfried Graf von Durckheim says, "When you're on a journey, and the end keeps getting further and further away, then you realize that the real end is the journey."

WISDOM

Real wisdom is sacred. Wisdom elicits an "Oh, yeah, of course," followed by, "Damn, I wish I'd thought of that."

I have a lot of Buddha quotes in this book (all of which, I think, are wise,) so it will come as no surprise that the first four quotes here are from him:

A fool who thinks that he is a fool is for that very reason a wise man. The fool who thinks that he is wise is called a fool indeed.

* * *

Once there was a man on a long journey who came to a river. He said to himself, "This side of the river is very difficult and dangerous to walk on, and the other side seems easier and safer, but how will I get across?" So he built a raft out of branches and reeds and safely crossed the river.

Then he thought to himself, "This raft has been very useful to me in crossing the river; I will not abandon it to rot on the bank, but will carry it along with me." And thus he voluntarily assumed an unnecessary burden. Can this man be called a wise man?

This parable teaches that even a good thing, when it becomes an unnecessary burden, should be thrown away.

* * *

Water is round in a round receptacle and square in a square one, but water itself has no particular shape. People often forget this fact.

* * *

A spoon cannot taste of the food it carries. Likewise, a foolish man cannot understand the wise man's wisdom even if he associates with a sage.

* * *

Before you can measure a thing, first you must know the measure.

♦ Yabo Saying

One day, when Mulla (the "Master") Nasrudin was sitting by the side of the road, a stranger came around the corner, greeted him, and asked, "How long will it take me to reach the nearest village?"

The Mulla returned the man's greeting pleasantly, then fell silent. Raising his voice the stranger repeated, "How long will it take me to reach the nearest village?" The Mulla smiled, but made no reply.

Frustrated, the stranger raised his voice again and shouted, "How long will it take me to reach the nearest village?" Again, Nasrudin smiled but said nothing. Muttering, "This man is either dead or a fool!" the stranger whirled on his heels and set off down the road with swift, angry strides.

Nasrudin watched him go. After several moments he called out thoughtfully, "It will take you nine minutes."

The stranger stopped. "Why didn't you say so before?" he demanded.

"How could I tell how long it would take you," replied the Mulla, "until I knew how fast you walked?"

♦ "Tales of Wisdom and Folly"

Si jeunesse savait, si vieillesse pouvait.
If youth knew, if old age could.

♦ French Saying

If you're going to bow, bow low.

♦ Eastern Wisdom

I LOVE this next one. It's a prescription for living with minimal angst.

If there is a way to overcome the suffering, then there is no need to worry; if there is no way to overcome the suffering, then there is no use in worrying.

♦ Shantideva, Indian Scholar

This is a quote from a Jim Jarmusch movie:

It is preferable not to travel with a dead man.

♦ Henri Michaux

Courage, Clarity and Humanity clear chaos from the mind.

♦ Robert Mirabel, Native American

Humility + Wonder = Wisdom

♦ Author Unknown

Yet I doubt not through the ages one increasing purpose runs,
And the thoughts of men will widen with the setting of the suns.

♦ Alfred Lord Tennyson, "Locksley Hall"

You think because you understand one you must understand two, because one and one makes two. But you must also understand *and.*

♦ Ancient Sufi Teaching

MAKING IT

There are many views of success. It's not so much which view is right, but more what you think success is. It's the same as deciding what wine you should like. I say taste them and choose the one you like. If the "experts" agree, terrific. If not, hey, it's your palette.

Many people spend their lives climbing the ladder of success only to find, when they get to the top, the ladder is leaning against the wrong building.

♦ Author Unknown

To laugh often and much; to win the respect of intelligent people and the affection of children; to earn the appreciation of honest critics and endure the betrayal of false friends; to appreciate beauty; to find the best in others; to have the world a bit better whether by a healthy child, a garden patch or a redeemed social condition; to know even one life has breathed easier because you lived; this is to have succeeded.

♦ Ralph Waldo Emerson

There ain't NO way to be out in front
Without showing your tail
To the horse behind.

♦ Langston Hughes

Satisfaction lies in the effort, not in the attainment. Full effort is full victory.

♦ Mahatma Gandhi

Life is a succession of moments
To live each one is to succeed.

♦ Corita Kent

One of our Management Training Seminars involved some executives who'd recently been rated "most successful" by their peers. At one point, we asked them to prioritize the 10 activities in their lives that gave them the greatest personal satisfaction and sense of self-worth. They didn't show these to anyone, simply put them down.

Then, we asked them to go over their lists and note the average number of hours or minutes they spent on each activity.

One man got so upset he nearly cried. Clearly, he already realized that he never seemed to have enough "free time" in his busy life. But what he hadn't focused on before was that the concept of success he'd pursued so diligently—and well—all his life apparently failed to include the things that mattered to him the most.

♦ F. Margolis

Second place is nothing but first loser.

♦ Michael Andretti

Only mediocre people are always at their best.

♦ Somerset Maugham

By the time we've made it, we've had it.

♦ Malcolm Forbes

You finally swim ashore and the bastards hit you over the head with a life jacket.

◆ Ernest Hemingway (on receiving the Nobel Prize)

What poor geometrician is there, but takes pride to be thought a conjurer? What mountebank would not make a living out of a false opinion that he were a great physician? And when many of them are once engaged in the maintenance of an error, they will join together for the saving of their authority to decry the truth.

◆ Thomas Hobbes

Money may be the husk of many things, but not the kernel. It brings you food, but not appetite; medicine, but not health; acquaintance, but not friends; servants, but not loyalty; days of joy, but not peace or happiness.

◆ Henrik Ibsen

THE PEOPLE WE CARE ABOUT

Relationships have to do with being connected and kinship. We are a relationship-prone species. We connect with each other in many ways—in pairs, families, clans, organizations, communities, and more.

If you were on your death bed, I doubt you'd be complaining that you hadn't spent more time at the office. On the other hand, you might well be saying you should have spent more time with the people you care about.

This section is a tribute to the people we care about.

A friend may well we reckoned
The masterpiece of nature.

    ♦ Ralph Waldo Emerson

What is a friend?
A single soul dwelling in two bodies.

    ♦ Aristotle

Here passed George MacDougal (*or any name you choose*)
With a twinkle in his eye,
The truth by his side,
Freedom in his bones,
Conviction in his heart,
And scorn for no man.

    ♦ Author Unknown

You would not be looking for me had you not already found me.

    ♦ Blaise Pascal

We are each of us angels with only one wing, and we can only fly embracing each other.

♦ Luciano DiCricenzo

This story shall the good man teach his son;
And Crispin Crispin shall ne'er go by,
From this day to the ending of the world,
But we in it shall be remembered;
We few, we happy few, we band of brothers;
For he today that sheds his blood with me
Shall be my brother; be he ne'er so vile,
This day shall gentle his condition:
And gentlemen in England now abed
Shall think themselves accursed they were not here,
And hold their manhoods cheap whiles any speaks
That fought with us upon Saint Crispin's day.

♦ William Shakespeare, "Life of King Henry V"

I open eye or ear, and stretch forth my hand, and feel in the same moment inseparably: Thou and I, I and Thou. At these moments the I is impossible without the Thou.

♦ Martin Buber (quoting Friedrich Heinrich Jacobi)

This is a poem from Mexico written in the Navajo style. The first line is meant to be repeated and meditated upon:

Only for a short time have you loaned us to each other.
Because it is in your drawing us that we take shape.
It is in your painting us that we get form.
It is in your singing to us that we get voice.
But only for a short while, have you loaned us to each other.
Because even as lines drawn in crystaline obsidian disappear
and as the green color of the Quetzalcoatal feathers fade
and as the waterfall subsides during the summer—so we too disappear.
Only for a short while have you loaned us to each other.

FOR SPECIAL ATTENTION:

"THE ALCHEMIST" by PAULO COELHO

My friend Anna Furlanis told me about Paulo Coelho. *I find his writing compelling and profound:*

"What's the world's greatest lie?" the boy asked.

"It's this: that at a certain point in our lives, we lose control of what's happening to us, and our lives become controlled by fate. That's the world's greatest lie."

* * *

For her, every day was the same, and when each day is the same as the next, it's because people fail to recognize the good things that happen in their lives every day that the sun rises.

* * *

"Isn't wine prohibited here?" the boy asked.

"It's not what enters men's mouths that's evil," said the alchemist. "It's what comes out of their mouths that is."

* * *

"Why are you called the alchemist?"

"Because that's what I am."

"And what went wrong when other alchemists tried to make gold and were unable to do so?"

"They were looking only for gold," his companion answered. "They were seeking the treasure of their destiny, without wanting actually to live out the destiny."

* * *

"Why do we have to listen to our hearts?" the boy asked, when they had made camp that day.

"Because, wherever your heart is, that is where you'll find your treasure."

* * *

Everything that happens once can never happen again. But everything that happens twice will surely happen a third time.

♦ Arab Proverb

* * *

The alchemist said, "No matter what he does, every person on earth plays a central role in the history of the world. And normally he doesn't know it."

I CANNOT EMPOWER YOU

The dictionary says that "empowerment" means "to give official authority or legal power to." But that's not the way the word is used today. Empowerment is a misunderstood buzzword. Sometimes a boss will say, "I empower you to do this," and what she really means is "Thank God it's off my back." Another time it will be said because it's the politically correct thing to say.

The basic misunderstanding about the notion of empowerment, though, is that it can be bestowed on someone, like a Knighthood. No! <u>The only person who can empower me is me.</u> Others can provide a conducive environment or atmosphere where I can function in an "empowered" or more responsible way. But if I don't want to be empowered, hearing "I empower you, Dan," is meaningless. Worse than that, it's a new burden I have to carry.

These quotes are more in keeping with what empowerment really is about.

The person who figures out how to harness the collective creative genius of the people in his or her organization is going to blow the competition away. And this takes entirely different skills from what it took to be a manager 15 years ago. You need an ego that permits you to believe that somebody else in your organization knows something. That's an acquired skill.

♦ Walter Wriston, Retired Chairman of Citicorp

Here are other versions of what Lao Tzu and Lao Tze say in "Follow the Leader:"

Tell me, I forget.
Show me, I remember.
Involve me, I understand.

♦ Chinese Proverb

Go to the people,
Learn from them,
Love them,
Start with what they know,
Build on what they have.
But of the best leaders
Their work is done
The people will remark
"We have done it ourselves"

♦ From a 2,000 year old Chinese poem

There is a man I know in Colombia who directed a community development organization. He observed one particular village to see what the most basic, most immediate needs of the children in this village were. The children were clearly undernourished, and what he decided they needed most was more food. He proposed that his organization work with the villagers to grow vegetables. Since there was unfarmed land available, it seemed as though there would be no problem.

As his organizers tried to bring the villagers together, though, they found there was no cooperation and no enthusiasm for the project. Finally, they sat down with the villagers and asked them what they thought the most important, most immediate needs of the children were (since they obviously didn't think it was to grow more vegetables.)

The villagers responded that what they needed most was a statue of the Virgin Mary near the school. For the children to go to a school where there wasn't a statue of the Virgin Mary "was not good!"

So, reluctantly at first, he and his organizers worked with the people to build a statue of the Virgin Mary on the top of a hill near the school. Some of the villagers donated sand, others collected and brought stones, others leveled the land at the top of the hill, and still others who knew something about masonry built the statue itself.

Almost unbelievably, the people worked in harmony to build the statue. Finally, when it was done, the villagers were so happy and so proud of what they had done—and they had enjoyed working together so much—that they looked to see what they could do next.

They knew their children's nutrition was important (albeit maybe not as important as the statue), so they began to level terraces on the hill in circles around the statue of the Virgin.   Then, after leveling the terraces, they planted vegetables so that their children could have a better diet.

♦ "The Statue of the Virgin Mary," as told to Andy Mason by Alvaro Villa

It becomes clear that to empower is purely an act of one's self, that it is unrelated to credit or taking credit, that no one ever "deserves" it; it can be only freely given, that there is no reason for it, nothing to "gain" by it, nothing to "get" out of it, no "pay-off," no motivation behind it, and it doesn't even make any sense—except in the realm of what we say we're about, in the realm of the "impossible"—and there it makes total sense, not because it is logical, but because it is obviously what's called for.

I've seen that something is being demanded, called for, some kind of total re-orientation of myself, some kind of complete redesign of what it means to be human.   And I see that the source of the "demand" is simply that the demand is there, appropriate, called up, needed.   Following instructions in this matter is totally insufficient—I must create this one myself, be responsible myself, take a stand myself, come to terms, very deeply and very personally, with what I have said I represent.

In that, there is freedom.

♦ Jack Mantos

Premise: Only you have the power to create context for yourself.
No one else has this power.

Paradox: Thought is largely collective

♦ Charles Smith

A coach is someone who makes you do what you don't want to do so you can be who you always wanted to be.

♦ Tom Landry

I don't agree with Landry, not only because he coached the Dallas Cowboys (which is reason enough), but because I don't think you can make somebody do what you want them to do. They are going to do what they want to do, and if it fits with your wants, terrific. You empower yourself.

HIT THE PAUSE BUTTON:

CANEK

I can't remember where I ran into "Canek, History and Legend of a Maya Hero," *by Emilio Abreu Gomez.* *I do remember I was intrigued by what Canek had to say, even when I didn't fully understand him.* *Here's a sampling:*

Canek said:

In a book I read an argument about what was the greatest thing in the world. Some philosophers said it was the water, others the mountains, others that it was the sun and somebody, I don't know who, said it was the disdain men could show for riches.

Doesn't it seem more right that the greatest thing in the world is not to disdain riches but to know how to make good use of them, so that the benefits don't rot in the hands of the wealthy or go to waste in the hands of incompetents.

* * *

Canek said:

By the very act of being, all beings have attributes, expressions of their essence, voices which reveal their origin and their condition. The attributes of being are not a decoration nor a quality which comes by chance from outside. The attribute is like the vapor from boiling water: it is water and not water. Thus the attribute of the sea is pride, the attribute of the sun authority, the attribute of men dignity.

* * *

Canek said:

Some prefer the ideal, others reality. From this results strife which festers in the spirit. Men never reconcile their points of view. The most they can do is to dream the reality or live the ideal. And the difference in desires goes on. But the men of this land ought to be both more demanding and more human. They ought to want the best reality—what is possible, what grows and ripens in their hands. That would be living the ideal of reality.

* * *

Canek said:

And why do you want liberty if you don't know how to be free? Liberty is not a gift which is granted or a right to be won. Liberty is a state of spirit. Once it has been created, then it is free even though it lacks freedom.

Irons and prisons can't stop a man from being free. To the contrary, they make him freer in the depths of his being. The freedom of a man is not like the freedom of a bird. The freedom of birds is satisfied by the to-and-fro rocking of a branch. Man's freedom is achieved in his conscience.

* * *

Canek said:

For the human spirit, a clean vice is worth more than a stained virtue. A clean vice can be a redeeming power. Hidden in it is an act of courage. On the other hand, stained virtue always implies weak desire. Certainly an act of cowardice.

THE CHILDREN AREN'T NESTLED ALL SNUG IN THEIR BEDS

At the Breakthrough Foundation, a non-profit organization I founded in 1980, we created and delivered a Youth at Risk Program. It was an intensive intervention in the lives of teenagers who were called "hard core juvenile delinquents." We worked with local volunteers in dozens of communities in the U.S. and beyond. Our clients were male and female gang members, drug users/dealers, killers, robbers, the works.

Youth at Risk forced us to confront what it means to be a child or teenager these days, especially a young person whose life is lived in the bowels of American cities. It's an ugly picture. And as Lois Haight Herrington *says, it affects each and every one of us, no matter where we live or what we do:*

Something insidious has happened in America. Crime has made victims of us all. Awareness of its dangers affects the way we think, where we live, what we do, what we buy, how we raise our children, and the quality of our lives as we age. The specter of violent crime and knowledge that without warning any person can be attacked or crippled, robbed or killed, lurk at the fringe of consciousness. Every citizen of this country is more impoverished, less free, more fearful and less safe because of the ever present threat of the criminal. Rather than alter a system that has proven incapable of dealing with crime, society has altered itself.

And more:

In 1988, I suggested to their mother, LaJoe, the possibility of my writing a book about Lafeyette, Pharoah, and the other children of the neighborhood. She liked the idea, although she hesitated and then said, "But you know, there are no children here. They've seen too much to be children."

♦ Alex Kotlowitz, "There Are No Children Here"

Our children are a mirror, an honest reflection of their parents and their world. Sometimes the reflection is flattering and at other times we simply don't like what we see. But we must never turn away.

♦ George Bush

In 1992 I was honored with an invitation from the Royal Society for the Arts, Manufactures and Commerce in London to deliver a lecture on our Youth at Risk Program. I accepted the invitation on behalf of the youth, volunteers and financial contributors who had made the program successful.

I began my talk with a quote about teenagers by one of England's own. This may have been written 400 years ago, but it sounds like an accurate current assessment to me:

I would there were no age between sixteen and three-and-twenty, or that youth would sleep out the rest; for there is nothing in the between but getting wenches with child, wronging the ancientry, stealing, fighting.

♦ William Shakespeare, "The Winter's Tale"

A slightly different perspective:

Every child is an artist. The problem is how to remain an artist once he grows up.

♦ Pablo Picasso

A twelve-year-old wants to be different than everyone else, the same as everyone else and accepted by all.

♦ E. L. Konigsburg

A child is a person who is going to carry on what you have started. He is going to sit where you are sitting and when you are gone, attend to those things which you think are important. You may adopt all the policies you please, but how they are carried out depends on him. He will assume control of your cities, your states, and your nation. He is going to move in and take over your churches, your schools, your universities, and your corporations. All your books are going to be judged, praised or condemned by him. The fate of humanity is in his hands.

◆ Abraham Lincoln

Morrise White *was a Youth at Risk Program participant from Los Angeles in 1987. He wrote:*

Until the eyes of self esteem are open,
There will be no true sight.
Until the voice of self motivation has spoken,
You cannot take action.
Until the listening of self control is heard,
You roam endlessly.
Until you master all these things,
You are useless to self, and to mankind.

Don't matter if anybody understand it or not. We just bringin' home the hate. That's the kind of world we live in.

◆ G-Roc, Gang Member in Los Angeles

What follows are three poems by inner city students. *I could just as easily have put them in the section on "Despair:"*

I am a wooden floor
that's being stepped on
and scraped so hard
that I can feel it
in my heart.

* * *

I fear death because I don't know
What will happen when I go.
It is something I can't face.
When I die, will I be thought about?
Will my name be shouted out?

* * *

I enter the race
To have material things,
To be rich,
To be loved by millions.
I am only human.
I do not fear death.
I fear life.

Daniel Ingham *was convicted and jailed for robbing a convenience store with a .22 caliber rifle. He was 19 years old when I met him. He wrote these two poems while participating in our Youth at Risk Program:*

IS THERE AN EASY WAY OUT

Is there an easy way out?
I'm pretty sure there must've been
cuz as I sit here with freedom gone
I know there was an easy way in.

"A way out of what?" you're asking me,
from a room that crowds you in,
the answers both are obvious
but we miss them again and again.

The "what" is your life that you've had until now
you've done both your best and your worst
but it's not the only one you have.
It's not your last, not even your first.

An easy way out, it doesn't exist
how easy can it be?
Like shedding skin, you can't begin
unless you've got new skin underneath.

If how you've lived has helped your life
and got you all you've needed
then ambition's gone, and that's all wrong
your purpose is defeated.

So if there's something else in life
you want but you're not getting
take a chance and try new ways
you can't win if you're not betting.

I AM FRIGHTENED

It is two in the morning,
The morning of the day when freedom will
once again be placed in my hands to do
with what I will and I am frightened...

Joy lays warm hands upon my heart,
A heart which has been suppressed and
shriveled with the passing time and I am frightened...

I feel the need to speak to my love,
Love of mother, love of father, love of
life and love of self and I am frightened...

I wonder about the dreams I've had,
dreams of struggle and pleasure
of failure and pain and still I am frightened...

I test and bend an inner strength,
A strength that seems new to me
yet impatiently tells me its been
here all along and I am frightened...
but less...

I cling to the handfuls of love and support,
Love and support that others give to me
but that I now know I can even give
unto myself and I am frightened...just a little

I see my life as a test,
A test to which I don't know all the answers
but that I must consistently take,
Even at times blindly guess but never
leave an answer blank and I am frightened...

I see a long line of excuses,
excuses that are clear and colorless and
only attempt but never succeed in
hiding the truth and can be removed
with courage and honesty and never
be missed and I am frightened or am I?

I see all these possibilities and I know
that I am my own master and it's time
for revolution because my old master is
weak. I see all this and I am frightened
not at all.

HIT THE PAUSE BUTTON:

"CREOLE PROVERBS OF BELIZE"

Belize is a small country down in Central America surrounded by Mexico, Guatemala and Honduras. I went there to do work with the Breakthrough Foundation. In their culture, straight talk is common.

During one of my trips I was given a book called "Creole Proverbs of Belize." *Here are some of them:*

- Rakatone da riba batam neba know sun hat.
  LITERALLY: Rokstone at river-bottom never knows the sun is hot.
  MEANING: Someone whose life is secluded cannot understand or be aware of many commonly known facts.

- Fishman neba seh e fish stink.
  LITERALLY: Fisherman never says his fish is stink.
  MEANING: Self-criticism is rare.

- Punkin neba bear water-melan.
  LITERALLY: The pumpkin vine never bears water-melons.
  MEANING: Children resemble parents.

- Empty crocus-beg kyaa(n't) 'tan up, an full crocus-beg kyaa(n't) bend.
  LITERALLY: Empty sacks can't stand upright; full ones can't bend.
  MEANING: Those who are hungry are weak and servile; those who are well-fed are arrogant.

- Wen cakroach mek dance, e no invite fowl.
  LITERALLY: When the cock-roach makes a dance, it doesn't invite the fowl.
  MEANING: Don't look for trouble.

- No call haligetta big-mout till you done cross the riba.
  LITERALLY: Don't call the alligator big-mouth till you have crossed the river.
  MEANING: Don't insult or defy those in whose power you are.

- Tiger maaga but e caca tarry.
  LITERALLY: The tiger is thin but its shit is sticky.
  MEANING: To say of a man "e caca tarry" generally indicates unexpected talent, especially qualities such as bravery and cunning.

- Sea-breeze blow pilikin same place e waa(n't) go.
  LITERALLY: The sea breeze blows the pelican in the same direction it wants to go.
  MEANING: When a person intends to do something, the unlikeliest circumstances serve as rationalizations.

- Horse weh no have horm no business eena cow gyallop.
  LITERALLY: Horses that don't have horns have no business in a race for cows.

- Wen fish come fram ribba-batam an' tell you haligetta gat a pain-a-belly, believe am.
  LITERALLY: When the fish comes from the river-bottom and tells you the alligator has a belly-ache, believe it.
  MEANING: Information obtained from someone in a position to know is likely to be true.

- The higher monkey climb, the more e expose (to danger).
  MEANING: High office is precarious.

- Ebry man know weh e own house leak.

    LITERALLY: Every man knows where his own house leaks.

    MEANING: We usually know our faults.

- Man weh get snake-bite run wen e see maklala.

    LITERALLY: The man who has had a snake bite runs when he sees a lizard.

    MEANING: Similar to "A burnt child dreads the fire" or Mark Twain's "A cat that has sat on a hot stove will not sit on a cold one."

- Wen rain come, jancrow say e wahn buil(d) house.

    LITERALLY: When rain comes, the carrion crow says it will build a house.

    MEANING: Be prepared for emergencies before they come.

- Da no one time monkey wa(nt) wife.

    LITERALLY: It's not once only that the monkey needs sexual intercourse.

    MEANING: Don't be ungrateful for favors received; you might need future favors.

- Pipple never stone empty mango tree.

    MEANING: To be criticized implies the possession of talent.

- Wen stone throw eena hag-pen, de hag weh squeal da de hag weh get lick.

    LITERALLY: When a stone is thrown into a hog-pen, the hog that squeals is the hog that gets hit.

    MEANING: When a general criticism is made, the person who resents it is often guilty of the fault.

- Kip you ass in line wid you heel.
  MEANING: Conduct yourself properly.

- Save you eye-water fo wen you ma dead.
  LITERALLY: Save your tears for when your mother dies.
  NOTE: Quoted when children (especially) cry over trifles.

- Blow your nose same place weh you ketch you cold.
  MEANING: When adversity comes, look for help from those who were your friends in prosperity (especially if they helped to cause the adversity.)

- Know how fu 'cratch groun' an no mek coco grow.
  LITERALLY: Know how to scratch the ground (i.e., till the soil) and not make coco (a tuber) grow.
  MEANING: To have one's pleasures and escape possibly unpleasant consequences (usually with a sexual implication.)

- Wen fire out, puppy rollin de ashes.
  MEANING: Misconduct appears when those in authority are absent.

- No ebryt'ing weh gat sugar sweet.
  LITERALLY: Not everything that has sugar is sweet.
  MEANING: What is tempting can prove disastrous.

- Wen sweet eena dog mout sour eena a bahin(d).
  LITERALLY: What is sweet in the dog's mouth is sour in his behind.
  MEANING: Pain often results from pleasure.

- Mek yourseld flo'-clot(h), pipple wipe de(m) foot pa(n) you.
  LITERALLY: (If you) make yourself a floor-cloth people will wipe their feet on you.

- Finger no say "look ya," e say "look deh."
  LITERALLY: Finger doesn't say "look here;" it says "look there."
  MEANING: We are readier to blame others than ourselves.

- As close as batty (ass) an' chamber (pot).

- Lia(r)d enough to lie the rust off cast iron.

- No heng you hat higher dan you can reach.
  MEANING: Make sure you can keep up with the cost of your lifestyle.

- Big da do(or) but coco da barrel.
  LITERALLY: Big at the door but (with only) coco (a small, inexpensive tuber) in the barrel.
  NOTE: Quoted to describe a person who is boastful and pretends to be important but is actually poor and insignificant.

- Gati, gati no wanti; a(nd) wanti, wanti no gati.
  LITERALLY: Got it, got it doesn't want it; and want it, want it hasn't got it.

- Big joota, small joota, same price—gi me the big joota.
  LITERALLY: Big shoes, small shoes, same price—give me the big shoes.

- Ev'rybody know weh de(m) own shoes pinch.

- One (bad) shot no spile de gun.
  MEANING: One mistake doesn't make a thing wholly bad. Quoted especially to show a woman can maintain or recover a good reputation after having had an illegitimate child.

- Cow caca pa(n) e tail, weh you expec(t) pa(n) de groun(d)?
  LITERALLY: (If) the cow shits on its tail, what do you expect on the ground?
  MEANING: A man who mistreats his own cannot be expected to treat strangers well.

THE THOUGHT POLICE

In "1984," Aldous Huxley talked about the Thought Police. In fact, I think each of us self-polices our thoughts. Our personal Thought Cop is on duty 24 hours a day, performing his duties as diligently when we're asleep as when we're awake.

He talks to us incessantly. He is what some people call the "little voice" in their head. And he has an opinion about everything. "I agree with that." "I don't agree with that." "She talks too much." "That's impossible. Why would anyone say something so stupid." Etc., etc., etc.

We listen to our Thought Cop's chatter and (mis)label it "me thinking." Well, it is "me," that's for sure. But is it really thinking?

I think that I never knew HOW to think. I feel as if I'm making it up as I go along. I don't know. At least, for the first time it's not making ME up.

♦ Martin Cruz Smith, "Gorky Park"

There are no dangerous thoughts; thinking itself is dangerous.

♦ Hannah Arendt

In order to think new thoughts or to say new things, we have to break up all our ready-made ideas and shuffle the pieces.

♦ Gregory Bateson

Practically, thinking means that each time you are confronted with some difficulty in life you have to make up your mind anew.

♦ Hannah Arendt

Here is the little voice in action:

Every revolutionary idea—in Science, Politics, Art or whatever—evokes three stages of reaction. They may be summed up by the three phrases:

1. It is impossible; don't waste my time.
2. It is possible, but it is not worth doing.
3. I said it was a good idea all along.

     ◆ Clarke's Law of Revolutionary Ideas

"Don't worry, white lady," said the slave. "You can forbid whatever you like, and I'll obey. The trouble is you can't forbid what I think."

     ◆ Gabriel Garcia Marquez, "Of Love and Other Demons"

FOLLOW THE LEADER

Everybody's got something to say about leaders and leadership, not much of it very useful. If you want evidence for my assertion, see how many great leaders you can find who became great leaders because of what they heard or read.

The trouble with "how to's" or "formulas" for success is that they don't prepare us for the unexpected. I think that great leadership has to do with being able to be great in the face of the unexpected, without losing the basic values or principles to which we are committed.

Maybe this is why I like my first quote so much. When Chesterton talks about furrowed fields that bend or the tough curves of the tree trunk or the foils that curve in the lunge I think he's talking about a basic component of leadership. There's something about the combination of strength, compassion and flexibility that come together in great leaders.

*When I look at the great leaders with whom I've been associated, something else stands out: **creativity**. Irrespective of the field or discipline in which they were working, they brought creativity into play as they faced difficult situations. And they weren't stuck with how it had to be or what had worked in the past.*

Leaders must offer uplifting, transcending leadership, a leadership of large ideas, broad direction, strong commitment.

♦ James MacGregor Burns

The great leader is seen as a servant first and that is the key to his greatness.

♦ Robert K. Greenleaf

Managers do things right. Leaders do the right thing.

- ♦ Warren Bennis

There is only one leader.

- ♦ Philip Knight, Chairman & CEO, Nike

(For what it's worth, I don't agree with Knight)

Most losing organizations are over-managed and under-led. Their managers accomplish the wrong things beautifully and efficiently.

- ♦ Joan Goldsmith & Warren Bennis, "Learning to Lead"

At the core of becoming a leader is the need always to connect one's voice and one's touch.

- ♦ Max DePree, CEO, Herman Miller, "Leadership Jazz"

The first responsibility of a leader is to define reality. The last is to say thank you. In between, the leader is a servant. *(Didn't Greenleaf say this?)*

- ♦ Max DePree, "Leadership is an Art"

The basic difference between an ordinary man and a warrior is that a warrior takes everything as a challenge, while an ordinary man takes everything as a blessing or a curse.

- ♦ Carlos Castaneda

It's clear from the poems by Lao Tze and Lao Tzu that they're either the same person or they skillfully "borrow" ideas from each other. In any event, I think they're both right:

The best of all rulers is but a shadowy presence to his subjects.
Next comes the ruler they love and praise;
Next comes one they fear;
Next comes one with whom they take liberties;
Hesitant, the best does not utter words lightly.
When his task is accomplished and his work done
The people all say, "It happened to us naturally."

♦ Lao Tze, "Tao Te Ching"

Fail to honor people,
They fail to honor you;
But of a good leader, who talks little,
When his work is done, his aim fulfilled,
They will all say, "We did this ourselves."

♦ Lao Tzu

Unless you are the lead dog, the scenery never changes.

♦ Author Unknown

You are greater than your deeds and truer than your surroundings.

♦ Rabindranath Tagore (in a letter to Jawaharlal Nehru)

Woe to people under a ruler without a sense of shame.

♦ Naguib Mahfouz, "Arabian Nights and Days"

Having listened to and read about Steve Jobs, I don't quite believe he means what he says here. Seems to me he is a very righteous guy. Nevertheless, what he says makes sense:

I don't care about being right. I care about being successful.

◆ Steve Jobs, Founder, Apple Computer

Leaders are the monitors, the keepers and shapers of an organization's assumptions. If we [leaders] don't challenge our most fundamental beliefs when they are in dire need of revision, then who will? Will it be our competitor who, unfettered by our history, can begin anew where we cannot?

◆ Ian Mitroff, "Break Away Thinking"

FOR SPECIAL ATTENTION:

"THE PROPHET" by KAHIL GIBRAN

It took me a long time to get around to Kahil Gibran. *I should have done it sooner.*

Love knows not its own depth until the hour of separation.

* * *

You give but little when you give of your possessions.

It is when you give of yourself that you truly give.

* * *

When you work you are a flute through whose heart the whispering of the hours turns to music.

* * *

The wind speaks not more sweetly to the giant oaks then to the least of all the blades of grass;

And he alone is great who turns the voice of the wind into a song made sweeter by his own loving.

* * *

Your joy is your sorrow unmasked.

* * *

The deeper that sorrow carves into your being, the more joy you can contain.

* * *

When you are sorrowful look again in your heart, and you shall see that in truth you are weeping for that which has been your delight.

* * *

Love has no other desire but to fulfill itself.

But if you love and must needs have desires, let these be your desires:

To melt and be like a running brook that sings its melody to the night.

To know the pain of too much tenderness.

To be wounded by your own understanding of love;

And to bleed willingly and joyfully.

To wake at dawn with a winged heart and give thanks for another day of loving;

To rest at the noon hour and meditate love's ecstasy;

To return home at eventide with gratitude;

And then to sleep with a prayer for the beloved in your heart and a song of praise upon your lips.

* * *

If you have only comfort, and the lust for comfort, that stealthy thing enters the house a guest, and then becomes a host, and then a master.

* * *

The lust for comfort murders the passion of the soul, and then walks grinning in the funeral.

* * *

Love one another, but make not a bond of love:

Let it rather be a moving sea between the shores of your souls.

Fill each other's cup but drink not from one cup.

Give one another of your bread but eat not from the same loaf.

Sing and dance together and be joyous, but let each one of you be alone,

Even as the strings of a lute are alone though they quiver with the same music.

Give your hearts, but not into each other's keeping.

For only the hand of Life can contain your hearts.

And stand together yet not too near together:

For the pillars of the temple stand apart,

And the oak tree and the cypress grow not in each other's shadow.

* * *

That which is boundless in you abides in the mansion of the sky, whose door is the morning mist, and whose windows are the songs and the silences of night.

* * *

The soul walks on all paths. The soul walks not upon a line, neither does it grow like a reed. The soul unfolds itself, like a lotus of countless petals.

* * *

Only when you drink from the river of silence shall you indeed sing.

And when you have reached the mountain top, then you shall begin to climb.

And when the earth shall claim your limbs, then shall you truly dance.

* * *

You have been told that, even like a chain, you are as weak as your weakest link.

This is but half the truth. You are also as strong as your strongest link.

To measure you by your smallest deed is to reckon the power of ocean by the frailty of its foam.

To judge you by your failures is to cast blame upon the seasons for their inconstancy.

BREAKING THROUGH

A breakthrough is not doing what you already know how to do, except better. It is not a step-by-step improvement. It is more a discontinuous leap, a state change. Going from liquid to solid, from water to ice, is a breakthrough.

Breakthroughs are too often seen as lucky accidents. You know, Mars and Venus lined up a certain way so a breakthrough was possible. Or as inevitabilities, so that after-the-fact they can be explained away as the inevitable result of what had gone before.

I think we can have something to do with making breakthroughs happen— without guarantees in advance, without previous experience. See "What's Possible" and "Taking a Risk" for clues.

I lived on the shady side of the road and watched my neighbors'
gardens across the way reveling in the sunshine.

I felt I was poor, and from door to door went with my hunger.

The more they gave me from their careless abundance the more I
became aware of my beggar's bowl.

Till one morning I awoke from my sleep at the sudden opening of
my door, and you came and asked for alms.

In despair I broke the lid of my chest open and was startled into
finding my own wealth.

   ♦ Rabindranath Tagore

Only those who have already experienced a revolution within themselves
can reach out effectively to help others.

   ♦ Malcolm X

One pioneering investigation into the essence of creativity studied the milestone contributions of 58 famous scientists and artists, including Einstein, Picasso and Mozart. They shared a common pattern: all breakthroughs occurred when two or more opposites were conceived simultaneously, existing side by side—as equally valid, operative and true. In an apparent defiance of logic or physical possibility, the creative person consciously embraced antithetical elements and developed these into integrated entities and creations.

♦ Author Unknown

A different kind of breakthrough:

Now that you have broken through the wall with your head, what will you do in the neighboring cell?

♦ S. J. Lec, "Unkempt Thoughts"

You gain strength, courage and confidence by every experience in which you really stop to look fear in the face. You must do the thing you think you cannot do.

♦ Eleanor Roosevelt

Where the pilgrimage ends is where the real journey begins.

♦ Charles Osgood

You should always go further than you should go.

♦ Jean Cocteau

Guitar: Wanna fly, you got to give up the shit that weighs you down.

♦ Toni Morrison, "Song of Solomon"

You can only force the Pony Express horse to go so fast. To go faster you need a telegraph.

♦ Lamar Alexander

FREE AT LAST

When I first went to India in 1962, India had been a free country for only 15 years. Indians had a different relationship to freedom than we do. We take freedom for granted. Maybe we think about it on the 4th of July. That wasn't the case in India in the 60's.

What I saw was that they created themselves as free people every day. Freedom was alive and tangible for them. It gave them great strength and courage, and it made freedom something special.

I learned that paying lip-service to our freedom isn't enough. Even though we have been free for centuries, we too can create our freedom newly any time we choose. Being aware of our freedom, having the experience of being free, makes it powerful and real.

Try it sometime.

The function of freedom is to free someone else.

♦ Toni Morrison

What does it matter, how many masters there are? There is only one slavery. Whoever refuses it is free, though the lords be legion.

♦ Ivan Klima, "Judge on Trial"

There are two kinds of exile. One kind is when you are banished from your home and have no chance of returning. The other is when you abandon yourself and are unable to return. The only advice I can give you is: don't confuse the two!

♦ Ivan Klima, "Judge on Trial"

Freedom is not free.

♦ Author Unknown

The bond of the slave is snapped the moment he considers himself to be a free being.

♦ Mahatma Gandhi

If—out of chaos—dancing stars of freedom.

♦ Jawaharlal Nehru (from a note to himself in 1942)

He alone is worthy of life and freedom
Who each day does battle for them anew.

♦ Goethe, "Faust" (Quoted by Andrei Sakharov in a famous essay)

We are afraid to give people freedom of choice because we are afraid they won't choose what we want them to choose.

♦ Werner Erhard

Maybe, Werner, but Stephen Muller has a slightly different take on it:

Amidst the glut of insignificance that engulfs us all, the temptation is understandable to stop thinking. The trouble is that unthinking persons cannot choose but must let others choose for them. But to fail to make one's own choices is to betray the freedom which is our society's greatest gift to all of us.

♦ Stephen Muller

If we cannot say what we think under our roof, then we have no roof.

    ◆ Arab Saying

THE PAST LIVES ON

The trouble with the future is that it will likely turn out to be very much like the past. Haven't you noticed how things tend to repeat themselves? Edna St. Vincent Millay *said:*

Life is not one thing after another,
It's the same damn thing over and over again.

And the French *say:*

Plus ca la change
Plus ca la meme chose
    or
The more things change
The more they stay the same

It isn't inevitable that the future will be a repetition of the past, but for that story you have to read "The Future Isn't Far Away." Here we're going to explore what a powerful grip the past has on us. *"The Calf Path,"* written by Sam Walter Foss in 1895, *is a perfect place to begin:*

One day through the primeval wood
A calf walked home as good calves should;
But made a trail all bent askew,
A crooked trail as all calves do.
Since then three hundred years have fled
And I infer the calf is dead.

But still he left behind his trail,
And thereby hangs my moral tale.
The trail was taken up next day
By a lone dog that passed that way;
And then a wise bellwether sheep
Pursued the trail o'er vale and steep.
And drew the flock behind him too,
As good bellwethers always do.
And from that day, o'er hill and glade,
Through those old woods a path was made.

And many men wound in and out,
And dodged and turned and bent about
And uttered words of righteous wrath
Because 'twas such a crooked path
But still they followed—do not laugh
The first migrations of that calf,
And through this winding wood-way stalked,
Because he wobbled when he walked
This forest path became a lane
That bent and turned and turned again;
This crooked lane became a road,
Where many a poor horse with his load,
Toiled on beneath the burning sun,
And traveled some three miles in one,
And thus a century and a half,
They trod the footsteps of that calf.

The years passed on in swiftness fleet
The road became a village street
And this, before men were aware,
A city's crowded thoroughfare.
And soon the central street was this
Of a renowned metropolis;
And men two centuries and a half
Trod in the footsteps of that calf.

Each day a hundred thousand rout
Followed the zigzag calf about.
And over his crooked journey went
The traffic of a continent.
A hundred thousand men were led
By one calf near three centuries dead.
They followed still his crooked way
And lost one hundred years a day;
For thus such reverence is lent
To well established precedent.

A moral lesson this might teach
Were I ordained and called to preach;
For men are prone to go it blind,
Along the calf-path of the mind,
And work away from sun to sun
To do what other men have done.
They follow in the beaten track
And out and in, and forth and back
And still their devious course pursue
To keep the path that others do
They keep the path a sacred groove,
Along which all their lives they move
But how the wise old wood-gods laugh
Who saw the first primeval calf.
Ah, many things this tale might teach
But I am not ordained to preach.

"The Calf Path" represents the structure of our thinking. We repeat the same behaviors and patterns without realizing how they began or how we keep them rooted in place. Usually it takes some cataclysmic event to shake us out of our patterns, but it doesn't have to be that way.

By seeing what's driving us we acquire the gift of choice. We can make our own decisions, not decisions dictated by the past. We can move from being the puppet dancing to the past's tune to the puppeteer pulling the strings.

But in the meantime, we see the past everywhere, especially when we look at how we think and communicate.

The two parties which divide the State, the party of Conservatism and that of Innovation, are very old. Now one, now the other, wins the day, and still the fight renews itself as if for the first time. It is the opposition of Past and Future, of Memory and Hope.

♦ Ralph Waldo Emerson

Habits and routine are great veils over our existence. As long as they are securely in place, we need not consider what life means; its meaning seems sufficiently incarnate in the triumph of daily habit. When social fabric is rent, however, man is suddenly thrust outside, away from habits and norms he once accepted automatically. There, on the outside, his questioning begins.

♦ Barrett

If you interact with a person based on your perception of them, fundamentally you'll be having a meeting with yourself.

♦ Jim Selman

If facts do not conform to the theory, they must be disposed of.

♦ Maier's Law

The world that we have made
As a result of the level of thinking we have done thus far
Creates problems we cannot solve
At the same level at which we created them.

♦ Albert Einstein

We can perceive the world only through our sense organs and our brain. But they have evolved in relation to only limited aspects of reality, not to the totality of creation.

♦ Rene DuBeau

The philosophy of the common man is an old wife that gives him no pleasure, yet he cannot live without her, and resents any aspersions that strangers may cast on her character.

♦ George Santayana

When society requires to be rebuilt, there is no use in attempting to rebuild it on the old plan. No great improvements in the lot of mankind are possible, until a great change takes place in the fundamental constitution of their modes of thought.

♦ John Stuart Mill

The only reason that we don't find solutions to our problems is because the answers interfere with our concepts.

♦ Sam Lewis

We often use the expression, "Seeing is believing." Nothing could be farther than the truth. In reality, unless something happens to jolt our belief system, what we see is determined by what we believe.

♦ Dorothy Gason

Our whole culture is concerned with establishing concepts and communicating them—but not with changing them. I know of no facet of education that examines the technique of changing or updating ideas. The tacit assumption is that it is enough to generate information, and that eventually the pressure of information will bring about a change in concepts. But experiments are designed, and the results are interpreted, in the light of the old concept.

♦ Edward de Bono

The mind resists contradictions and suppresses information that does not support a decision already made.

♦ Festinger's Theory of Cognitive Dissonance

To rest upon a formula is a slumber that, prolonged, means death.

♦ Oliver Wendell Holmes, Jr.

Men are not prisoners of fate, but only prisoners of their own minds.

♦ Franklin D. Roosevelt

Your position offered as a position is a contribution. Your position offered as the truth is pure venom.

♦ Ron Smotherman

Thinking only begins at the point where we have come to know that reason, glorified for centuries, is the most obstinate adversary of thinking.

♦ Martin Heidegger

Every man takes the limits of his own field of vision for the limits of the world.

♦ Arthur Schopenhauer

Our vision of science as a practice grounded in objectivity omits, George Johnson *reminds us, the influence of the observer on what is being studied. This is from* "In the Palaces of Memory:"

Wherever one decides to draw the line between the subjective and the objective, it is clear that we don't stand outside creation like gods, with the power to describe the world with perfect objectivity.

It is not just that we affect what we observe by the very act of observation; the world is filtered through our senses, and the information is processed and sorted into patterns by our brains. We only see light in a tiny band of the electromagnetic spectrum. We see what our nervous system allows us to see.

The universe would be a very different place for a creature whose brain was wired according to another blueprint, who sampled the world through portals we can only imagine. Science, then, is not a description of the physical world, but a description of how the world interacts with the mind—and how experience is translated into the structures we call memories.

The greatest danger in times of turbulence is not the turbulence; it is to act with yesterday's logic.

♦ Peter Drucker

What terrifies us about death is not the loss of the future but the loss of the past.

♦ Milan Kundera, "The Book of Laughter and Forgetting"

227

People are always shouting they want to create a better future. It's not true. The future is an apathetic void of no interest to anyone. The past is full of life, eager to irritate us, provoke and insult us, tempt us to destroy or repaint it. The only reason people want to be masters of the future is to change the past.

♦ Milan Kundera, "The Book of Laughter and Forgetting"

People usually prefer to remember than to think.

♦ Shimon Peres

It is historical continuity that maintains most assumptions—not a repeated assessment of their validity.

♦ Edward de Bono

The past is never dead. It is not even past.

♦ William Faulkner

The only way history answers questions is by putting further questions.

♦ Karl Marx

Misapprehensions about the past have a way of determining the future.

♦ David Kearns/David Nadler, "Prophets in the Dark"

Man is not restricted by things, but by his opinion of things.

♦ Epictetus

It is never too late to give up our prejudices.

♦ Henry David Thoreau

Loyalty to petrified opinion never yet broke a chain or freed a human soul.

♦ Mark Twain

The world is full of people whose notion of a satisfactory future is, in fact, a return to an idealized past .

♦ Robertson Davies, "The Cunning Man"

We are only what we remember, nothing more...all we have is the memory of what we have done or not done; whom we might have touched, even for a moment.

♦ Romesh Gunesekera, "Reef"

In life one must put blinders on, look straight ahead, and above all, learn to forget. You cannot live and be your own pawnbroker.

♦ Andre Aciman, "Out of Egypt"

The future is the present wearing yesterday's shoes.

♦ Author Unknown

NOW HEAR THIS

There are overlaps in this book. For example, some of the ideas here could be in "The Past Lives On" or in "I Already Know That." But how we listen is unique unto itself, so it gets to be it's own thing.

We're not very good listeners. In fact, we're terrible listeners. As Suzuki says, we're usually listening to ourselves. We're trained to speak. We take classes in Public Speaking. We should take classes in Public Listening. Our attention is on our speaking, i.e, on ourselves. Yet, how we listen and how others listen to us has more impact on real communication than speaking does.

When you listen to someone, you should give up all your preconceived ideas and your subjective opinions; you should just listen to him, just observe what his way is. Usually when you listen to some statement, you hear it as a kind of echo of yourself. You are actually listening to your own opinion. If it agrees with your opinion you may accept it, but if it does not, you will reject it or you may not even really hear it.

♦ Shunryu Suzuki

Sometimes if both people are willing to listen carefully, it is possible to do more than exchange greetings and good wishes. Even to do more than exchange information. The two people may even find out something which neither of them knew before.

♦ Gregory Bateson

An official who must listen to the pleas of clients should listen patiently and without rancor, because a petitioner wants attention to what he says even more than the accomplishing of that for which he came.

♦ Pharoah Ptahotep, 2400 BC

Got to do more than speak. You got to be moving toward the heart of the matter, got to burn people's souls. You got to get inside of people. That's where it all is. And you can't get inside of them unless you open yourself up to be got inside of. The key to other people's hearts is finding the key to yours.

♦ Jesse Jackson

If you don't say anything, you won't be called on to repeat it.

♦ Calvin Coolidge

Didn't they call him Silent Cal?

Flies can't enter closed mouths.

♦ Spanish Proverb

But each ear is listening to its hearing, so none hear.

♦ W.H. Auden

I listen with an intensity most people reserve for speaking.

♦ Lily Tomlin

Perhaps what I have to listen to is more important than what I have to say.

♦ Steven Covey

Seek first to understand, then to be understood.

◆ Steven Covey

Look for you yesterday/Here you come today
Your mouth wide open/But what you got to say?

◆ Amiri Baraka

There are pieces of them in there...I hear them screaming.

◆ Coffey, in Stephen King's, "The Green Mile," as he walks past the
electric chair

FOR SPECIAL ATTENTION:

"THE TIBETAN BOOK OF LIVING & DYING"
by
SOGYAL RINPOCHE

My fascination with the Himalayas began as a child when I saw the movie, "Lost Horizons," the Shangri-la story. In 1959 I remember hearing that the Dalai Lama had fled from Tibet through the Himalayas to India. Then, in 1963, I met groups of Tibetan refugees who had followed the Dalai Lama to India.

This work by Sogyal Rinpoche *was my first serious introduction to Tibetan Buddhist philosophy. While I don't relate well to strict dogma or rigorous practice in Buddhism or any other religion, I do relate to the suggestions of how to see and live life that I find in Buddhist writings. Certainly as expressed by Sogyal Rinpoche and the Dalai Lama, there is a tolerance and appreciation of other views that I find refreshing.*

I recommend "The Tibetan Book of Living and Dying" *in its entirety. In the meantime:*

We do not know where death awaits us: so let us wait for it everywhere. To practice death is to practice freedom. A man who has learned how to die has unlearned how to be a slave.

♦ Montaigne

The birth of a man is the birth of his sorrow. The longer he lives, the more stupid he becomes, because his anxiety to avoid unavoidable death becomes more and more acute. What bitterness! He lives for what is always out of reach! His thirst for survival in the future makes him incapable of living in the present.

♦ Chuang Tzu

Confined in the dark, narrow cage of our own making which we take for the whole universe, very few of us can even begin to imagine another dimension of reality. Patrul Rinpoche tells the story of an old frog who had lived all his life in a dank well. One day a frog from the sea paid him a visit.

"Where do you come from?" asked the frog in the well.

"From the great ocean," he replied.

"How big is your ocean?"

"It's gigantic."

"You mean about a quarter of the size of my well here?"

"Bigger."

"Bigger? You mean half as big?"

"No, even bigger."

"Is it . . . as big as this well?"

"There's no comparison."

"That's impossible! I've got to see this for myself."

They set off together. When the frog from the well saw the ocean, it was such a shock that his head just exploded into pieces.

* * *

Tomorrow or the next life—which comes first, we never know.

♦ Tibetan Saying

Remember the example of an old cow,
She's content to sleep in a barn.
You have to eat, sleep, and shit—
That's unavoidable—
Beyond that is none of your business.

♦ Patrul Rinpoche

The disciple asked his master:

"Master, how do you put enlightenment into action? How do you practice it in everyday life?"

"By eating and sleeping," replied the master.

"But Master, everybody sleeps and everybody eats."

"But not everybody eats when they eat, and not everybody sleeps when they sleep."

From this comes the famous Zen saying, "When I eat, I eat; when I sleep, I sleep."

♦ Zen Story

When your fear touches someone's pain it becomes pity; when your love touches someone's pain, it becomes compassion.

♦ Stephen Levine

Grief can be the garden of compassion.

♦ Rumi

To see a World in a Grain of Sand
And a heaven in a Wild Flower
Hold Infinity in the palm of your hand
And Eternity in an hour.

♦ William Blake

For as long as space exists
And sentient beings endure,
May I too remain,
To dispel the misery of the world.

Lord make me an instrument
Of thy peace, where there is hatred,
Let me sow love;
Where there is injury, pardon;
Where there is doubt, faith;
Where there is despair, hope;
Where there is darkness, light;
And where there is sadness, joy.
O Divine Master, grant that
I may not so much seek
To be consoled as to console;
To be understood as to understand;
To be loved as to love;
For it is in giving that we receive,
It is in pardoning that we
Are pardoned, and it is in dying
That we are born to eternal life.

♦ Author unknown

I have shown you the way to liberation, now you must take it for yourself.

♦ Buddha

Some day, after we have mastered the winds, the waves, the tides and gravity...we shall harness...the energies of love. Then, for the second time in the history of the world, man will have discovered fire.

♦ Teilhard de Chardin

JUST BECAUSE I LIKE THEM

The definition of a fanatic:

Someone who, having lost sight of his objective, redoubles his efforts.

♦ George Santayana

We [journalists] cover revolution better than we cover evolution.

♦ James Reston

The definition of insanity:

Doing the same thing over and over again, expecting different results.

♦ Rita Mae Brown

Noise proves nothing. Often a hen who has merely laid an egg cackles as if she laid an asteroid.

♦ Mark Twain

The course of the avalanche depends on the stones over which it rolls.

♦ Czeslaw Milosz

Every answer is a form of death.

♦ John Fowles

My experience is that when things are non-controversial, beautifully coordinated and all the rest, it must be that there is not much going on.

- ♦ John F. Kennedy

A conclusion is a place where you got tired of thinking.

- ♦ Fischer's Law

An Irishman doesn't know what he thinks until he's in an argument with another Irishman.

- ♦ George Bernard Shaw

If you think you're too small to have an impact, try going to bed with a mosquito.

- ♦ Author Unknown

Especially if you're both inside the mosquito net.

The uncreative mind can spot wrong answers, but it takes a creative mind to spot wrong questions.

- ♦ Antony Jay, "Management and Machiavelli"

I am trying to cultivate a life-style that does not require my presence.

- ♦ Garry Trudeau

How can I move forward when I don't know which way I'm facing?

- ♦ Author Unknown

For unto whomsoever much is given, of him shall be much required: and to whom men have committed much, of him they will ask the more.

> ◆ Luke 12:48

Because we are different provides the possibility for harmony—like an orchestra.

> ◆ Sufi Saying

The origin of mountain streams is like the origin of tears: patent to the understanding, but mysterious to the sense.

> ◆ Mary Austin

Healing is possible even when a cure in not.

> ◆ Doctor (working with cancer patients)

I don't know where to put this quote. I can interpret it as cynicism and despair; I can interpret it as possibility; I can interpret it as the way life is. I'll leave it up to you.

Everything is poison; nothing is poison.

> ◆ Haitian Saying

It is the weak who are cruel. Gentleness can only be expected from the strong.

> ◆ Leo Roskin

This is for anyone who (like Dan of yesteryear) is scornful of business:

Seest thou a man diligent in his business? he shall stand before kings.

♦ Proverbs 22:29

This quote is from a billboard on Sunset Blvd. in Hollywood in the middle 50's. If I recall correctly, it was on the lawn of a church.

The difference between a rut and a grave is only a matter of depth.

♦ Author Unknown

Whenever I watch TV and see those poor starving kids all over the world, I can't help but cry. I mean I'd love to be skinny like that but not with all those flies and death and stuff.

♦ Mariah Carey

Right, Mariah. You're all heart.

Television is how we dream out loud about ourselves.

♦ John Leonard

CYNICISM AND ITS BROTHER, DESPAIR

I know we have a dark side, but I resist empowering it. I reject cynicism and despair. I can appreciate why they might arise, (see Anjek below) but I still reject them. Not for me! Cynicism and despair put us in a prison from which we cannot escape. They put us behind the Walls of No Hope.

If you could lick my heart it would poison you.

♦ Anjek

Anjek was featured in a movie about the Holocaust. He had been a leader of Jewish resistance in the Warsaw ghetto. Many years later his life was one of pure, concentrated bitterness. The saddest part is that even though he lived, his torturers won.

I worry that humanity has been 'advanced' to its present state of incompetency because evolution works on the Peter Principle.

I worry that our lives are like soap operas. We can go for months and not tune into them, then six months later we look in and the same stuff is still going on.

I worry about whoever thought up the term 'quality control,' who thought if we didn't control it, it would get out of hand. I worry no matter how cynical you become—it's never enough to keep up.

♦ Lily Tomlin, "The Search for Signs of Intelligent Life in the Universe"

Mankind is a skin disease on the face of the earth.

♦ William Bullitt, Former US Ambassador to the USSR

Wouldn't you love to have Bullitt as your dinner partner.

If people bring so much courage to this world the world has to kill them to break them, and then, of course, it kills them. It kills the very good and the very gentle and the very brave, impartially. (If you are none of these you can be sure that it will kill you too, but there will be no special hurry.)

     ♦ Ernest Hemingway

Well, he showed 'em. He killed himself first.

Tomorrow, and tomorrow, and tomorrow,
Creeps in this petty pace from day to day
To the last syllable of recorded time.
And all our yesterdays have lighted fools
The way to dusty death. Out, out brief candle!
Life's but a walking shadow, a poor player
That struts and frets his hour upon the stage,
And then is heard no more. It is a tale
Told by an idiot, full of sound and fury,
Signifying nothing.

     ♦ William Shakespeare, "Macbeth"

This is brutal. Maybe I should have canned this section.

If I could, I would emit the darkness inside me like a squid and blind them all and run.

     ♦ Robert Stone, "Children of Light"

Men have died from time to time and worms have eaten them, but not for love.

     ♦ Robert Stone, "Children of Light"

Great tasks are rarely achieved by cynics.

   ♦ Henry Kissinger

Yeah, right, Henry. It takes one to know one. You tell 'em.

This couplet was spoken by Gerda Mannfreed, *a Holocaust survivor, as she observed (on film) her sick and dying fellow prisoners being freed:*

Noble be man
Merciful and good

   ♦ Goethe, "The Divine"

Maybe quiet, private despair is the worst:

The majority of people perform well in a crisis and when the spotlight is on them; it's on the Sunday afternoons of this life, when nobody is looking, that the spirit falters.

   ♦ Alan Bennett, "Writing Home"

The happiest of lives are only splendid wrecks of what used to be a future.

   ♦ Gore Vidal, "Palimpsest"

To understand hell we must examine the paradise from which it originated.

   ♦ Milan Kundera (*a paraphrase of what he said*)

I'm not really sure if this poem by Yeats is what it seems to be on the surface, which is pretty despairing. But since he was Irish, and in the absence of any other insight—it goes here:

Turning and turning in the widening gyre
The falcon cannot hear the falconer;
Things fall apart; the centre cannot hold;
Mere anarchy is loosed upon the world,
The blood-dimmed tide is loosed, and everywhere
The ceremony of innocence is drowned;
The best lack all conviction, while the worst
Are full of passionate intensity.

Surely some revelation is at hand;
Surely the Second Coming is at hand.
The Second Coming! Hardly are those words out
When a vast image out of i{Spiritus Mundi}
Troubles my sight: somewhere in sands of the desert
A shape with lion body and the head of a man,
A gaze blank and pitiless as the sun,
Is moving its slow thighs, while all about it
Reel shadows of the indignant desert birds.
The darkness drops again; but now I know
That twenty centuries of stony sleep
Were vexed to nightmare by a rocking cradle,
And what rough beast, its hour come round at last,
Slouches toward Bethlehem to be born?

 ♦ William Butler Yeats, "The Second Coming"

The world in which we live can be understood as a result of muddle and accident, but if it is the outcome of a deliberate purpose, the purpose must have been that of a fiend.

 ♦ Bertrand Russell

What was justice? Justice was revenge wrapping itself in a cloak of high principle.

 ♦ Ivan Klima, "Waiting for the Dark, Waiting for the Light"

If you bit your tongue you would poison yourself.

♦ Gabriel Garcia Marquez, "Of Love and Other Demons"

Marquez should get together with Anjek and Robert Stone.

If the people lead, eventually the leaders will shoot them.

♦ Bumper Sticker (also on the same car: "Honor Union Labor")

Life is hard, and then you die. Then they put you in a hole in the ground. Then they put dirt on you and bury you. Then a dog comes and pisses on your grave. And nobody cares. Too bad for you.

♦ Author Unknown

Now—aren't you glad this section's over? I am.

HIT THE PAUSE BUTTON:

INSURANCE EXPLANATIONS

The following are actual statements from insurance claims in which drivers were asked to summarize the details of their accidents in the fewest words possible:

- Coming home I drove into the wrong house and collided with a tree I don't have.

- The other car collided with mine without giving warning of it's intentions.

- I thought my window was down, but I found it was up when I put my head through it.

- I collided with a stationary truck coming the other way.

- A truck backed through my windshield into my wife's face.

- A pedestrian hit me and went under my car.

- The guy was all over the road. I had to swerve a number of times before I hit him.

- I pulled away from the side of the road, glanced at my mother-in-law and headed over the embankment.

- In my attempt to kill a fly, I drove into a telephone pole.

- I had been shopping for plants all day and was on my way home. As I reached an intersection, a hedge sprang up, obscuring my vision and I did not see the other car.

- I had been driving for 40 years when I fell asleep at the wheel and had an accident.

- I was on my way to the doctor with my rear end trouble when my universal joint gave way causing me to have an accident.

- As I approached the intersection a sign suddenly appeared in a place where no sign had ever appeared before. I was unable to stop in time to avoid the accident.

- To avoid hitting the bumper of the car in front of me, I struck a pedestrian.

- My car was legally parked as it backed into the other vehicle.

- An invisible car came out of nowhere, struck my car and vanished.

- I told the police that I was not injured, but on removing my hat found I had a fractured skull.

- I was sure the old fellow would never make it to the other side of the road when I struck him.

- The pedestrian had no idea which direction to run, so I ran over him.

- I saw a slow moving, sad faced old gentleman as he bounced off the roof of my car.

- The indirect cause of the accident was a little guy in a small car with a big mouth.

- I was thrown from my car as it left the road. I was later found in a ditch by some stray cows.

- The telephone pole was approaching, and I was attempting to swerve out of it's way when it struck the front end.

CHALLENGING THE STATUS QUO

Vested interests will fight tooth and nail to preserve their turf. And it won't be a clean fight.

I have mixed feelings on this one. On the one hand, I like the idea of challenging the status quo: the fat, comfortable, privileged group. On the other hand, I don't see the point of challenging for the sake of challenging. Being against everything that's in place makes no sense to me.

Men fear thought as they fear nothing else on earth—more than ruin—more even than death. Thought is subversive and revolutionary, destructive and terrible, thought is merciless to privilege, established institutions, and comfortable habit. Thought looks into the pit of hell and is not afraid. Thought is great and swift and free, the light of the world and the chief glory of humanity.

    ♦ Bertrand Russell

A sense of potential and a sense of riddance are the two poles of American liberty.

    ♦ George Santayana

Daring as it is to investigate the unknown, even more so it is to question the known.

    ♦ Kaspar

We have it in our power to begin the world over again.

    ♦ Thomas Paine

Every person with an ideal faces the danger of being called a fool or a madman. Every great cause must be ushered into the world by a small minority of persons often denounced as cracked brains or ridiculous zealots. Someone said, "Nobody can be genuinely in earnest without appearing eccentric in the world where intensity is considered bad form."

♦ Rev. Paul Osumi

God help us to change
To change ourselves and to change our world
To know the need for it
To deal with the pain of it
To feel the joy of it
To undertake the journey without understanding the destination
The art of gentle revolution

Amen

♦ Michael Leunig, "A Common Prayer"

Any attempt at ontological interpretation, that is, any attempt to get at a "way of being" constantly has the character of doing violence, whether to the claims of the everyday interpretation, or to its complacency and its tranquilized obviousness.

♦ Martin Heidegger

The most intimidating status quo for me to challenge, of course, is me:

To have doubted one's own first principles is the mark of a civilized man.

♦ Oliver Wendell Holmes, Jr.

He who cannot change the very fabric of his thoughts will never be able to change reality.

♦ Anwar Sadat

And so, for the first time in my life, perhaps, I took the lamp, and I went down to my inmost self. But as I moved further and further from the conventional certainties, I became aware that I was losing contact with myself. At each step of the descent a new person was disclosed within me... and when I had to stop my exploration because the path faded, I found a bottomless abyss at my feet, and out of it came—arising I know not whence—the current which I dare to call my life.

♦ Teilhard de Chardin

MAKING LEMONADE

*This is about: if you are expecting oranges and you get lemons, don't cry,
make lemonade.*

I'm a real perfectionist. But that's the irony. In order to do it perfectly I
have to let go of perfection a little. For instance, in diving, there's a "sweet
spot" on the board, right at the end. I can't always hit it perfectly.
Sometimes I'm a little back from it. Sometimes, I'm a little over, but the
judges can't tell that.

I have to deal with whatever takeoff I have been given. I can't leave my
mind on the board. I have to stay in the present. I have to be relaxed
enough to clue into my memory tape of how to do it. That's why I train so
hard, not just to do it right, but to do it right from all the wrong places.

♦ Greg Louganis

Sorrow happens, hardship happens,
The hell with it.
Who never knew the price of happiness will not be happy.

♦ Yevgeny Yevtushenko

People are always blaming their circumstances for what they are. I don't
believe in circumstance. The people who get on in this world are the people
who get up and look for the circumstances they want, and if they can't find
them, make them.

♦ George Bernard Shaw, "Mrs. Warren's Profession"

Failure is the opportunity to begin again more intelligently.

♦ Henry Ford

257

It's not easy bein' green.

♦ Kermit the Frog

SEEING IS BELIEVING

I'm batting. The ball comes toward me at unbelievable speed. It's the size of a pea. It's in the catcher's mitt before I can swing the bat. But for someone else, the ball looks as big as a watermelon coming across the plate in super slo-mo. Why?

I don't know. Let's attribute it to genes; it's mom's and dad's fault. That doesn't lessen the frustration though.

I talked with Joe (Montana) about how baseball players say they're in the 'zone,' when the ball seems to move in slow motion. What's it like to be in the pocket? I ask—that eye of the hurricane, with so much frantic energy colliding around him.

"Well, it feels like it's slowing down, but I think it's more like all of a sudden it gets crystal clear. It's wide open, and there doesn't seem to be anything in your way. Or if there is, you can see everything around."

Does that feeling come and go? I ask.

"You don't even realize that it's happening until usually after a game," Joe replies. "You sit back and think about plays, and all of a sudden, it feels like the line parts and you can see the whole field. Almost even directly to your sides, your peripheral vision. All the vision that you want. Sometimes it happens that way, and other times," he chuckles, "there are a lot of people in front of you."

♦ Gary Kamiya

Yeah, but when I'm really red hot, the ball looks like it's coming at me in slow motion, and hitting then becomes a little like bowling. It's like I'm the seven pin—the corner pin in back—and this bowling ball is rolling down the lane. When you've got everything working, that's how big and slow pitches look coming up to the plate. Everything happens in a split second, of course, but when I'm really on a tear, I can actually see the ball hit the bat, the bat recoil and the ball leave the bat.

◆ Keith Hernandez

A change of pace for a different kind of seeing:

I wondered how it was possible to walk for an hour through the woods and see nothing of note. I who cannot see find hundreds of things: the delicate symmetry of a leaf, the smooth skin of a silver birch, the rough, shaggy bark of a pine.

I who am blind can give one hint to those who see: use your eyes as if tomorrow you will have been stricken blind. Hear the music of voices, the song of a bird, the mighty strains of an orchestra as if you would be stricken deaf tomorrow. Touch each object as if tomorrow your tactile sense would fail. Smell the perfume of flowers, taste with relish each morsel, as if tomorrow you could never taste or smell again. Make the most of every sense.

Glory in all the facets and pleasures and beauty which the world reveals to you.

◆ Helen Keller

The beauty is in the walking.
We are betrayed by destinations.

◆ Gwyn Thomas

And yet another kind of seeing:

If the doors of perception were cleansed everything would appear to man as it is, infinite.

For man has closed himself up, til he sees all things thro' narrow chinks of his cavern.

♦ William Blake, "The Marriage of Heaven and Hell"

Behavior comes out of how a player sees things. If he sees a tennis ball as a threat, he swings as if he's defending himself, and he does 33 wrong things. See what he sees before you start coaching.

The great coaches look behind behavior and address what drives behavior. They use conversation to change perceptions.

♦ Tim Gallwey

From nothing in the field of sight can it be concluded that it is seen from an eye.

♦ Ludwig Wittgenstein

When you seek something, you only see the thing that you are seeking. You only think about the thing you are seeking. When you are obsessed with your goal, you do not see many things that are under your nose.

♦ Herman Hesse, "Siddartha"

To see is to wait to receive that which chooses to reveal itself.

♦ Alan Jones, Dean of Grace Cathedral, San Francisco

If I didn't see it with my own mind I wouldn't believe it.

♦ Author Unknown

HUMANITY - SHOWING OUR BEST SIDE

I trust that given a chance people will show their best side. I may be disappointed from time to time, but that is no excuse for giving up on my assumption. When I work with people I really do trust them to be great, and they usually are. Our challenge, of course, is to behave this way with the people who are closest to us. Tell the truth now: isn't it easier to be magnanimous with acquaintances than with those we love?

When we create an environment or an atmosphere where the best can emerge, what appear to be miracles happen. They are not miracles, of course, they are simply people being themselves, i.e., being great.

Forgiveness is not an occasional act, it is a permanent attitude.

   ♦ Martin Luther King, Jr.

Good fortune will elevate even petty minds, and give them the appearance of a certain greatness and stateliness, as from their high place they look down upon the world; but the truly noble and resolved spirit raises itself, and becomes more conspicuous in times of disaster and ill fortune.

   ♦ Plutarch

I expect to pass through this life but once. If therefore there be any kindnesses I can show, or any good thing I can do to any fellow beings, let me do it now. Let me not defer or neglect it, for I shall not pass this way again.

   ♦ A.B. Hegeman

FOR SPECIAL ATTENTION:

ANTOINE de ST. EXUPERY AGAIN

If you know St. Exupery's *writings you know that his range of insights transcends any one book and any one subject. All the quotes below are from,* "Wartime Writings" *and they clearly demonstrate his breadth. I could have put each of these quotes in other places, but somehow I like seeing what he has to say all in one place. Enjoy!*

I admire science, but I also admire wisdom.

* * *

It is not enough to cut into a man's heart in order to save him—he must be touched by grace. It is not enough to prune a tree in order to make it bear fruit—spring must come too. It is not enough to lighten the plane's cargo—there must be a sea breeze as well.

* * *

True freedom lies only in the creative process. The fisherman is free when he fishes according to his instinct. The sculptor is free when carving a face. It is a travesty of freedom to be free to choose between four models produced by General Motors, or between three films by Zanuck, or between the twelve items offered at a drugstore.

* * *

A cathedral is built with stones; it is made up of stones; but the cathedral ennobles each stone, which becomes a cathedral stone. In the same way, you will only find brotherhood in something larger than yourselves, because one is a brother "in" something, not merely a brother. People need to find a bond between them.

* * *

The "trick" is sacrifice. And by sacrifice I mean neither renunciation of all the good things of life nor despair in repentance. By sacrifice I mean a free gift, a gift that demands nothing in return. It is not what you receive that magnifies you, but what you give. That which you give to the community builds the community, and the existence of the community enriches your own substance.

* * *

One silence differs from another.

There is the tranquil silence when the tribes are at peace, when night brings coolness and one seems to be anchored with furled sails in a quiet harbor.

There is the midday silence when the sun suspends all thought and movement.

There is the deceptive silence when the north wind bears down, bringing insects borne like pollen from the oases of the interior and heralding the advent of a sandstorm from the east.

There is the silence of conspiracy when it is known that a distant tribe is preparing to revolt.

There is the silence of mystery when the Arabs are gathered together for one of their secret meetings.

There is the pregnant silence when the messenger is late in returning, the shrill silence when in the night one holds one's breath in order to hear, the melancholy silence when one remembers one's beloved.

* * *

In order for human beings to be free, they must first be human.

* * *

A rose isn't a succession of stages.   A rose is a faintly melancholy celebration.

ART

I wish I had more on art. Alas... this and Paul Chelko's section are it.

The only thing that matters in art is the part that cannot be explained.

   ♦ Georges Braque

A great painting teaches us nothing.
It raises and refreshes the spirit—that's all.

   ♦ Rado

Humility in the artist is his frank acceptance of all experiences, just as Love in the artist is simply that sense of Beauty that reveals to the world its body and its soul.

   ♦ Oscar Wilde

You make too much music. A raga is not composed of notes. It is composed of the silence between the notes.

   ♦ Gita Mehta, "The River Sutra"

When you ask me what I came to do in this world, as an artist I will answer you: I came to live out loud.

   ♦ Emile Zola

If you don't love the blues, you've got a hole in your soul.

   ♦ Jimmy Rogers, Chicago Blues Singer

Good artists copy; great artists steal.

♦ Pablo Picasso

I know I'm not going to be here forever. I just want to contribute something that will last forever.

♦ Illinois Jacquet, Jazz Musician

My music is evidence of my soul's will to live.

♦ Charles Mingus, Jazz Musician

Trying to describe a work of art is like trying to cut roast beef with a screwdriver.

♦ Author Unknown

The creative act is emotion recollected in tranquillity.

♦ William Wordsworth

There is something on the earth that is free of everything but what created it, and that is the one thing that I have been trying to find.

♦ Ornette Coleman, Jazz Musician

The creative process is nothing but a series of crises.

♦ Isaac Bashevis Singer

THERE IS SOMETHING NEW
UNDER THE SUN

I'm intrigued by what it takes to solve difficult problems. Often the solutions come when I suddenly see something that had been invisible but was there all the time. I may have puzzled over a picture that seemed like an abstract design until, in a magical instant, I see a clear image embedded in it.

For years I've enjoyed doing the New York Times Sunday crossword puzzle. (In ink, of course; pencils are for wimps.) I am often stumped for a long time, but almost always, even though it may be frustrating and seemingly hopeless, if I stay with it long enough I'll see ways to solve it. I don't understand how this phenomenon works. Maybe it has something to do with staying with the question longer than usual.

Einstein's way (below) makes a lot of sense to me. He combines the new with the traditional in a way that others can see the point. That's practical as well as creative.

Most people would agree that Einstein's ideas were really new—despite his disclaimer. They were new not because they contained new ingredients but because they embodied a whole new set of rules for making the cake. "What was new with Einstein was his approach," says Wheaton. "Others came very close, but they all thought you could fiddle around with Newtonian laws and save the assumptions. Einstein saw that Newton's fundamental assumptions were open to question."

Truly new ideas not only build on tradition; they also break with it. But there's a catch to this definition of a new idea. As Wheaton points out, "If an idea is truly new, it generally won't be accepted."

Einstein got around this catch by making certain his ideas had measurable results. "He never wrote a paper," says Wheaton, "that didn't spell out what experiments you could perform to prove whether or not his theory was true." Einstein followed it through. And in the end, that is the true mark of ownership of any idea. That is, it's fine to have ideas, but they are not really yours until you do something with them.

   ♦ K.C. Cole

Creativity is contagious—pass it on.
A person who never made a mistake never tried anything new.
Creativity is shaking hands with tomorrow.
Creativity is singing in your own key.
Creativity is digging deeper.
Creativity is plugging into the sun.

   ♦ Author Unknown

Most of the universe is composed of invisible material of an unknown kind.

   ♦ From a New York Times article, 1/5/93, about invisible, "dark", matter that may halt expansion of the universe.

Right! Now I understand.

If we do not expect the unexpected it will never happen.

   ♦ Heraclitus

A problem solver tries to make something go away. A creator tries to bring something new into being

   ♦ Peter Senge

Man's mind, once stretched by a new idea, never regains its original dimensions.

♦ Oliver Wendell Holmes, Jr.

The real act of discovery consists not in finding new lands
But in seeing with new eyes.

♦ Marcel Proust

Ideas are themselves substantive with the power to influence and even transform human life. In effect, ideas are not unlike food, vitamins, or vaccines. They invoke inherent potential for growth and development and can effect the course of evolution.

♦ Dr. Jonas Salk

With me each day that dawns begins a new year. I have no memories.

♦ James Michener, "Hawaii"

HOW TIMELY

Time gets a bad rap. We're always blaming time for something:
- *If I only had more time*
- *Some other time*
- *It's time we talked*
- *Time out*

It's time we changed our relationship with time. Let's make time our ally, not our enemy.

How old would you be if you didn't know how old you was?

♦ Satchel Paige

Time is the floating image of eternity.

♦ Plato, "The Timaeus"

We [Japanese] have a saying that time has no single measure, that time can be like frost or lightning or a tear or sigh or storm or sunset or even like a rock.

♦ James Clavell, "Shogun"

Gaijin do not understand time as we do, they do not consider or think about time as we do. They think time is finite. We do not. They worry about time, minutes, hours, days, months are important to them, exact appointments sacrosanct. Not to us. Their version of time controls them. So this is one cudgel we can always use to beat them with.

♦ James Clavell, "Gaijin"

Time is an equal opportunity employer. Each human being has exactly the same number of hours and minutes every day.

♦ Denis Waitley, "The Joy of Working"

I am coming to feel that the people of ill will have used time much more effectively than the people of good will. We will have to repent in this generation not merely for the vitriolic works and actions of the bad. people, but for the appalling silence of the good people.

We must come to see that human progress never rolls in on wheels of inevitability. It comes through the tireless efforts and persistent work of men willing to be coworkers with God, and without this hard work itself becomes an ally of the forces of social stagnation. We must use time creatively, and forever realize that the time is always ripe to do right.

♦ Martin Luther King, Jr.

We are always getting ready to live. But there is never time for living.

♦ Ralph Waldo Emerson

Hours are artificial constructs; moments are not.

♦ Michael Ventura

Life is not made of years; it is made of moments.

♦ Elie Wiesel

As they say, "Great minds think the same way," or something like that.

Time takes time

♦ Author Unknown

How sour sweet music is
When time is broke and no proportion kept!
So is it in the music of men's lives.

I wasted time, and now doth time waste me;
For now hath time made me his numbering clock;
My thoughts are minutes.

♦ William Shakespeare, "Richard II"

FOR SPECIAL ATTENTION:

"MAN'S SEARCH FOR MEANING"
by
VIKTOR FRANKL

I've rarely read a book with the power and profound impact of "Man's Search for Meaning." *Primo Levi is the only other person I've read who has written about his personal experiences inside the Holocaust with such honesty and humanity. Here is some of what* Viktor Frankl *has to say:*

Man can preserve a vestige of spiritual freedom, of independence of mind, even in terrible conditions of psychic and physical stress.

* * *

Everything can be taken from a man but one thing: the last of the human freedoms—to choose one's attitude in any given set of circumstances, to choose one's own way.

* * *

We refused to minimize or alleviate the camp's tortures by ignoring them or harboring false illusions and entertaining artificial optimism.

* * *

Schopenhauer: Mankind is apparently doomed to vacillate eternally between the two extremes of distress and boredom.

* * *

What man actually needs is not a tensionless state but rather the striving and struggling for some goal worthy of him. What he needs is not the discharge of tension at any cost, but the call of a potential meaning waiting to be fulfilled by him...the feeling that life is meaningful.

Sometimes the frustrated will to meaning is vicariously compensated for by a will to power, the will to money...the will to pleasure.

* * *

They had nothing more to expect from life. It was a question of getting them to realize that life was still expecting something from them. We need to stop asking about the meaning of life, and instead think of ourselves as those who are being questioned by life—daily and hourly.

* * *

Human existence is essentially self-transcendence rather than self-actualization.

* * *

I could not change his fate...I did succeed in changing his attitude toward his unalterable fate.

* * *

The burden of unavoidable unhappiness is increased by unhappiness about being unhappy.

* * *

My comrades' question was, "Will we survive the camp? For, if not, all this suffering has no meaning." The question which beset me was, "Has all this suffering, this dying around us, a meaning?" For, if not, then ultimately there is no meaning to survival; for a life whose meaning depends upon such a happen-stance—whether one escapes it or not—ultimately would not be worth living at all.

* * *

Man constantly makes his choice concerning the mass of present potentialities; which of these will be condemned to nonbeing and which will be actualized?

* * *

To be sure, a human being is a finite being, and his freedom is restricted. It is not freedom from conditions, but freedom to take a stand toward the conditions.

* * *

An erroneous and dangerous assumption is the view of man that disregards his capacity to take a stand toward any conditions whatsoever. Man is not fully conditioned and determined; he determines himself whether to give in to conditions or stand up to them. In other words, man is ultimately self-determining. Man does not simply exist, but always decides what his existence will be, what he will become in the next moment.

By the same token, every human being has the freedom to change at any instant...One of the main features of human existence is the capacity to rise above such conditions and transcend them...A human being is a self-transcending being.

* * *

Ultimately, man should not ask what the meaning of his life is, but rather must recognize that it is he who is asked. In a word, each man is questioned by life; and he can only answer to life by answering for this own life; to life he can only respond by being responsible.

JUST BECAUSE I LIKE THEM

When it comes to exercise, I engage in sleeping and resting. I never could see any benefit in being tired. And when an impulse to exercise settles down upon my spirit, I quickly lie down until it goes away.

♦ Mark Twain

What got him was nothing and nothing's exactly what anyone living or somebody dead like even a poet could hardly express, what I mean is what knocked him over wasn't for instance the knowing your whole yes goddamned life is a flop or even to feel how everything dreamed and hoped and prayed for months and weeks and days and years and nights and forever is less than nothing which would have been something. What got him was nothing.

♦ e.e. cummings

Amoz Oz, *the Israeli writer, is a marvelous storyteller. These quotes are from his book,* "Fima":

The main thing an old cat remembers is how to meow.

♦ Bulgarian Proverb

* * *

The difference between a shlemiel and a shlemazel: the shlemiel spills his tea and it always lands on the shlemazel.

* * *

If the light within you darkens, it is written, how great is the darkness.

* * *

His place does not know him.

◆ Biblical Phrase

* * *

You've forgotten yourself.

* * *

My soul droops with sorrow.

◆ Psalms

* * *

The most wretched fate was not to be forgotten but, precisely, to fade away.

* * *

"The rabble soon assembled
Bearing the noose of blame,
To hang the King and Council
And free themselves from shame."

That is more or less the bottom line of all history.

◆ Alterman, "Songs of the Plagues of Egypt"

Darjeeling is in northeastern India. Mention Darjeeling to some people and they'll think of tea. Others will think of the British Raj hill station, where the colonial administration went to escape the heat. I worked in Darjeeling quite a bit in the 1963-65 period when I was living in Calcutta. For me, Darjeeling is about Tibetan refugees and extraordinary views of the Himalayas.

On a recent trip to Darjeeling I noticed that some wonderful things were written on the walls in a shopping area. I copied down a few:

Friendship is a rainbow between two hearts.

* * *

What was wonderful about childhood is that anything in it was a wonder.

* * *

The true use of speech is not so much to express our wants as to conceal them.

* * *

Don't wait for the 11th hour, because you may die at 10:30.

HIT THE PAUSE BUTTON:

"BUDDHA'S LITTLE INSTRUCTION BOOK"
by
JACK KORNFIELD

This book is a gold mine.

- Love in the past is only a memory. Love in the future is a fantasy. Only here and now can we truly love.

- To give your cow or sheep a large, spacious meadow is the best way to control him.

- If you can't find the truth right where you are, where else do you think you will find it?

- In the beginner's mind there are many possibilities, in the expert's mind there are few.

- Live like the strings of a fine instrument—not too taut and not too loose.

- If your compassion does not include yourself, it is incomplete.

- Everything in moderation, including moderation.

- There is only one time when it is essential to awaken. That time is now.

- It is not our preferences that cause problems but our attachment to them.

- The trouble is that you think you have time.

- If you do not care for each other, who will care for you?

- No matter how difficult the past, you can always begin again today.

- When asked, "Are you a god or a man?" the Buddha replied, "I am awake."

- Not getting what you desire and getting what you desire can both be disappointing.

- That which is timeless is found now.

- Don't keep searching for the truth, just let go of your opinions.

- Joy and openness come from our own contented heart.

- As you walk and eat and travel, be where you are. Otherwise you will miss most of your life.

- To know the way and not practice is to be a soup ladle in the pot and not taste the flavor of the soup.

- Fear is always an anticipation of what has not yet come.

- Without mercy for ourselves we cannot love the world.

- Things to do today: Exhale, inhale, exhale. Ahhhh.

- If you wish to know the divine, feel the wind on your face and the warm sun on your hand.

- Those who are awake live in a state of constant amazement.

JUST BECAUSE I LIKE IT:

CHIEF SEATTLE

In 1852, the United States Government inquired about buying tribal lands. Chief Seattle, speaking for his people, wrote the following letter:

The President in Washington sends word that he wishes to buy our land. But how can you buy or sell the sky? The land? The idea is strange to us. If we do not own the freshness of the air and the sparkle of the water, how can you buy them?

Every part of this earth is sacred to my people. Every shining pine needle, every sandy shore, every mist in the dark woods, every meadow, every humming insect. All are holy in the memory and experience of my people.

We know the sap which courses through the trees as we know the blood that courses through our veins. We are part of the earth and it is part of us. The perfumed flowers are our sisters. The bear, the deer, the great eagle, these are our brothers. The rocky crests, the juices in the meadow, the body heat of the pony, and man, all belong to the same family.

The shining water that moves in the streams and rivers is not just water, but the blood of our ancestors. If we sell you our land, you must remember that it is sacred. Each ghostly reflection in the clear waters of the lakes tells of events and memories in the life of my people. The water's murmur is the voice of my father's father.

The rivers are our brothers. They quench our thirst. They carry our canoes and feed our children. So you must give to the rivers the kindness you would give any brother.

If we sell you our land, remember that the air is precious to us, that the air shares its spirit with all the life it supports. The wind that gave our grandfather his first breath also receives his last sigh. The wind also gives our children the spirit of life. So if we sell you our land, you must keep it apart and sacred, as a place where man can go to taste the wind that is sweetened by the meadow flowers.

Will you teach your children what we have taught our children? That the earth is our mother? What befalls the earth befalls all the sons of the earth.

This we know: the earth does not belong to man, man belongs to the earth. All things are connected like the blood that unites us all. Man did not weave the web of life, he is merely a strand in it. Whatever he does to the web, he does to himself.

One thing we know: our god is also your god. The earth is precious to him and to harm the earth is to heap contempt on its creator.

Your destiny is a mystery to us. What will happen when the buffalo are all slaughtered? The wild horses tamed? What will happen when the secret corners of the forest are heavy with the scent of many men and the view of the ripe hills is blotted by talking wires? Where will the thicket be? Gone! Where will the eagle be? Gone! And what is it to say goodbye to the swift pony and the hunt? The end of living and the beginning of survival.

When the last Red Man has vanished with his wilderness, and his memory is only the shadow of a cloud moving across the prairie, will these shores and forests still be here? Will there be any of the spirit of my people left?

We love this earth as a newborn loves its mother's heartbeat. So, if we sell you our land, love it as we have loved it. Care for it as we have cared for it. Hold in your mind the memory of the land as it is when you receive it. Preserve the land for all children and love it, as God loves us all.

As we are part of the land, you too are part of the land. This earth is precious to us. It is also precious to you. One thing we know: there is only one God. No man, be he Red Man or White Man, can be apart. We are brothers after all.

GETTING OFF THE HOOK - OR NOT

Being responsible in life is not many things:
- *It's not "mea culpa"*
- *It's not weltschmerz (look it up)*
- *It's not Jewish guilt*
- *It's not some burden I've got to carry*
- *It's not "I've got to be a big person and own up to this"*
- *Etc.*

Ok, fine, you say. If that's what responsibility isn't, then what is it?

*Responsibility begins with choice. Being responsible is when I've freely chosen what I say I'm responsible for; nobody made me do it. And it goes both ways: If I can freely choose to be responsible, I can freely choose **not** to be responsible. There is freedom and power in the choosing.*

A caveat: In living life as a responsible person you may expect others to behave responsibly. That's a mistake. You'll then have to deal with your disappointment, anger, frustration, and the like when it doesn't happen. But what others do or don't do doesn't get you off the hook. Sorry.

There is a tendency today to absolve individuals of moral responsibility and treat them as victims of social circumstances. You buy that, you pay with your soul.

It's not men who limit women, it's not straights who limit gays, it's not whites who limit blacks. What limits people is lack of character. What limits people is that they don't have the fucking nerve or imagination to star in their own movie. Let alone direct it. Yuk!

♦ Tom Robbins, "Still Life with Woodpecker"

I've gone back and forth about whether to include "Invictus." One, I love obscure quotes, and it's not obscure enough to elicit a "Wow, I've never heard that before." Two, it could have been written by Job; man, this guy's really had it tough. The clincher, though, was that after re-reading it (many times) it seems to be a genuinely responsible statement. So—here it is.

Out of the night that covers me
Black as the pit from pole to pole
I thank whatever God may be
For my unconquerable soul
In the fell clutch of circumstances
I have not winched, not cried aloud
Under the blogions of chance
My head is bloody but unbowed
Beyond this place of wrath and tears
Looms but the horror of the shade
And yet the menace of the years
Finds and shall find me unafraid
It matters how straight the gate
How charged with punishment the scroll
I am a master of my fate
I am the captain of my soul.

 ♦ William Henlay, "Invictus"

I am pleased at having taken on so many obligations. In my life most curious elements accumulated: gentle ghosts which undid me, an insistent mineral labor, an inexplicable wind which ruffled me, the stab of some wounding kisses, the hard reality of my brothers, my insistent need to be always watchful, my impulse to be myself, only myself in the weakness of self pleasuring.

That is why—water on stone—my life was always singing between joy and obligation.

 ♦ Pablo Neruda

Dear God, are we doing the right thing or are we just jerking off?

> ◆ Mel Brooks, "Blazing Saddles" (movie)

I think it's a mistake to ever look for hope outside of one's self. One day the house smells of fresh bread, the next of smoke and blood. One day you faint because the gardener cut his finger off, within a week you're climbing over corpses of children bombed in a subway. What hope can there be if that is so?

I tried to die near the end of the war. The same dream returned each night until I dared not to sleep and grew quite ill. I dreamed I had a child, and even in the dream I saw it was my life, and it was an idiot, and I ran away. But it always crept into my lap again, clutched at my clothes. Until I thought, if I could kiss it, whatever in it was my own, perhaps I could sleep.

And I bent to its broken face, and it was horrible...but I kissed it. I think one must finally take one's life in one's arms.

> ◆ Arthur Miller, "After the Fall"

I love/hate what Arthur Miller says. Each time I read it I am both horrified and drawn to it. I want the result, but I want there to be an easier way. I'm afraid there might not be an easier way, and it pisses me off. Too bad for me, I guess.

We first raise the dust and then claim we cannot see.

> ◆ George Berkeley

The price of greatness is responsibility.

> ◆ Winston Churchill

I am under the impression that in nine out of ten cases I deal with windbags who do not fully realize what they take upon themselves, but who intoxicate themselves with romantic sensations.

From a human point of view this is not very interesting to me, nor does it move me profoundly. However, it is immensely moving when a mature man—no matter whether old or young in years—is aware of a responsibility for the consequences of his conduct and really feels such a responsibility with heart and soul.

He then acts by following the ethic of responsibility and somewhere he reaches a point where he says: Here I stand; I can do not other. That is something genuinely human and moving. And every one of us who is not spiritually dead must realize the possibility of finding himself at some time in that position.

◆ Max Weber

It is not for you to complete the work, but neither are you free to desist from doing it.

◆ Rabbi Tarfon

He who cannot dance will say:
"The drum is bad."

◆ Ashanti Proverb

You can no more choose than you can fly while falling.

◆ John Leonard (referring to addiction)

I don't agree with Leonard on this one. No responsibility. No choice. No life.

Accountability is taking responsibility before the fact, rather than after the fact.

It is taking a stand, and standing by it.

When those who are accountable are right, they take the credit. When they're wrong, they take the heat.

It's a fair exchange.

Accountability is a way of working.

Those who practice it have an unspoken respect for each other.

And a visible disdain for the absentminded apologizers, mumbling excuse-makers, and trembling fence-sitters who run from integrity as if it were the plague.

♦ Shearson/Lehman/American Express

The only thing necessary for the triumph of evil is for good men to do nothing.

♦ Edmund Burke

FINDING THE ENEMY

If we're looking for the source of hostility in our lives, we would be smart to look in the mirror before we point at others.

There is nothing more detestable than a man who runs away from his demon.

♦ Joseph Conrad, "Heart of Darkness"

Hell is the state in which we are barred from receiving what we truly need because of the value we give to what we merely want.

♦ Jacob Needleman, "Money & The Meaning of Life"

Our chief want in life is somebody who will make us do what we can.

♦ Ralph Waldo Emerson

Sorry, Ralph my man, that somebody is you.

Wars end. Hostilities go on forever.

♦ Pablo Picasso

If you can dream and not make dreams your master;
If you can think and not make thoughts your aim;
If you can meet with triumph and disaster and
   treat those two impostors just the same...

♦ Rudyard Kipling

For all of us our own particular creature lurks in ambush.

♦ Hugh Walpole

The Lord set his heart in love upon your father and chose their descendants after them, you above all peoples, as at this day. Circumcise therefore the foreskin of your heart, and be no longer stubborn.

♦ Deuteuronomy 10:12-16

Resentment is just a way of letting someone else use your mind rent-free.

♦ Roger Ebert

Why do you want light if you're blind?

♦ Mingrelian Proverb

There is a terrible emptiness in me, an indifference that hurts.

♦ Albert Camus, "The First Man"

If there is no enemy within, the enemy without can do us no harm.

♦ Author Unknown

HIT THE PAUSE BUTTON:

FLIP WILSON

Flip Wilson tells this story. It's a great example of the power of communication—or the lack of it:

A guy came home from a trip and asked the gardener how things went while he was away:

Gardener: Everything went fine, Mr. Austin.
Mr. Austin: Nothing at all to report?

Gardener: Well, you may not know that the dog died.
Mr. Austin: That's terrible. How did he die?

Gardener: He died when he went to the barn to see what was wrong with the horse.
Mr. Austin: What was wrong with the horse?

Gardener: He was suffocating.
Mr. Austin: Suffocating?

Gardener: Yes, Mr. Austin.
Mr. Austin: Why was he suffocating?

Gardener: He was suffocating from the smoke.
Mr. Austin: Where was the smoke coming from?

Gardener: From the barn.
Mr. Austin: Was the barn on fire?

Gardener: Yes.
Mr. Austin: How did the barn catch fire?

Gardener: From the sparks.
Mr. Austin: Sparks?

Gardener: Yes, from the sparks.
Mr. Austin: Where did the sparks come from?

Gardener: From the roof of the house.
Mr. Austin: Was the roof burning?

Gardener: Yes, Mr. Austin.
Mr. Austin: What caused the roof to burn?

Gardener: The drapery caught fire from the candles, so the house started to burn.
Mr. Austin: Candles? We don't have any candles in the house.

Gardener: The candles were brought in specially.
Mr. Austin: Why?

Gardener: To be put around the corpse.
Mr. Austin: Corpse? What corpse?

Gardener: The corpse was your mother.
Mr. Austin: My mother is dead? How did she die?

Gardener: From a heart attack.
Mr. Austin: What caused her to have a heart attack?

Gardener: It was when she heard what happened.
Mr. Austin: What did she hear happened?

Gardener: She heard your wife had run away with the mailman, and she died.

FOR SPECIAL ATTENTION:

DAVID WHYTE AGAIN

These quotes are from a talk David Whyte *gave in London in May 1995. It is called* "The Intelligent Organization."

Advice an elder gives to a child who asks: "What do I do when I'm lost in the forest?:"

Stand still. The trees ahead and the bushes beside you are not lost.
Wherever you are is called "here."
And you must treat it as a powerful stranger,
Must ask permission to know it and be known.
Listen, the forest breathes, it whispers, "I have made this place around you.
If you leave it you may come back again saying 'here.'"
No two trees are the same to raven.
No two branches are the same to wren.
If what a tree or a branch does is lost on you,
Then you are surely lost.
Stand still.
The forest knows where you are.
You must let it find you.

Whyte's comment: People are living their lives second hand. They are sleepwalking. How do you know where you belong? You need to be alert in the world. There is silence in this poem. We need to have a silence in us to perceive the world.

I am certain of nothing but the holiness of the heart's affections and the truth of the imagination.

    ♦ John Keats

One day you finally knew what you had to do
And began though the voices around you kept shouting their bad advice
Though the whole house began to tremble
And you felt the old tug at your ankles
"Mend my life," each voice cried, "Mend my life. Mend my life."
But you didn't stop, though the wind pried with its stiff fingers at the very
        foundations, though their melancholy was terrible
It was already late enough and a wild night and the road full of fallen
        branches and stones
But little by little as you left their voices behind
The stars began to burn through the sheets of clouds
And there was a new voice
Which you slowly recognized as your own
That kept you company as you strode deeper and deeper into the world
Determined to do the only thing you could do
Determined to save the only life you could save

    ♦ Mary Oliver, "The Journey"

Whyte's comment: We're all afraid of the world today. Are you willing to
come alive in this world?

What is time but eternity living dangerously.

    ♦ Irish Philosopher

From David Whyte:

- Question: How is the change process going in your organization?
  Answer: We're in a stage of advanced lip service.

- To deal with change you have to deal with the feeling of betrayal.

- We're used to being on the path, where we can get coordinates to tell us where we are. But now we are operating in the wilderness, where there are no coordinates and we need wilderness skills; we need to know how to live off the land. Need to know who you are, especially in relationship to the world.

- Empowerment in the workplace is moving from a parent-child relationship (that we grew up with) to a peer-peer relationship, an adult relationship, where we see that there is a lot at stake for you as well as me.

- How do you remember who you are as a human being? How do you give your particular gift to the organization you're working for?

- How do you live in a world where your identity is at stake?

Next is a fragment of a poem by Robert Frost, *called* "Two Tramps in Mudtime." *The tramps are trying to sort out what life is really about:*

Yield who will to their separation
My object in living is to unite my avocation and my vocation
As my two eyes make one insight
Only where love and need are one
And work is play for mortal stakes
Is the deed ever really done for heaven and the future's sake.

Whyte's comment: We should use all our faculties to see.

That day I saw beneath dark clouds the passing light over the water
And I heard the voice of the world speak out
I knew then, as I had before, life is no passing memory of what has been
Nor the remaining pages in a great book waiting to be read
It is the opening of eyes long closed
It is the vision of far off things seen for the silence they hold
It is the heart after years of secret conversing
Speaking out loud in the clear air
It is Moses in the desert fallen to his knees before the lit bush
It is the man throwing away his shoes as if to enter heaven
And finding himself astonished
Opened at last
Fallen in love with solid ground

♦ David Whyte, "The Opening of Eyes"

TAKING A RISK

I tend to consider how risky something is after I've done it. Looking back I think, "I would have been intimidated had I given that any real thought." And then I'm glad I did it. Getting out on the edge, beyond your comfort zone, is a great way to surprise yourself about yourself.

For some of us, physical risks are easier than other kinds of risks. For example, a sky diver may be terrified at the thought of getting into a relationship. And vice versa. We're either going to let our fears determine how far we go or acknowledge that our fears are there and go ahead anyway.

Believing you can be perfect is the fatal imperfection.
Believing you're invulnerable is the ultimate vulnerability.
Being a warrior doesn't mean winning or even succeeding. But it
does mean putting your life on the line. It means risking and
failing and risking again, as long as you live.

♦ George Leonard, "Warriors"

Being on the tightrope is living;
Everything else is waiting.

♦ Karl Wallenda

For three straight months prior to his San Juan walk, all Karl thought about was falling. He put all his energies into not falling rather than walking the tightrope.

♦ Karl Wallenda's wife, talking about his fatal fall.

No noble thing can be done without risks.

> ♦ Montaigne

Our lives can be an accident or an adventure. The choice is ours.

> ♦ Norm Howe

Half a revolution is not enough. It may even be worse than no revolution at all.

> ♦ James Champy

Security is mostly a superstition.
It does not exist in nature.
Nor do the children of men as a whole experience it.
Avoiding danger is no safer in the long run than outright exposure.

Life is either a daring adventure or nothing.

> ♦ Helen Keller

Progress always involves risk. You can't steal second base and keep your foot on first base.

> ♦ Frederick Wilcos, Ballplayer

By not daring to take the risks of making something happen, management takes, by default, the greater risk of being surprised by what will happen. This is the risk that even the largest and richest company cannot afford to take.

> ♦ Peter Drucker

To be is to be vulnerable.

♦ Norman O. Brown

No one ever travels so high as he who knows not where he is going.

♦ Oliver Cromwell

If you can't run with the big dogs, don't get off the porch.

♦ James Barksdale, CEO

All daring starts from within.

♦ Eudora Welty

We must not cease from exploration
And the end of all our exploring
Will be to arrive where we began
And to know the place for the first time.

♦ T.S. Eliot, "Little Gidding"

Guitar: If a man don't *have* a chance, then he has to *take* a chance.

♦ Toni Morrison, "Song of Solomon"

If we knew beforehand where we were going to fall, we could lay down a mattress.

♦ Russian Proverb

Be brave enough
To live creatively.
The creative is the place
Where no one else has ever been.
You have to leave the city of your comfort
and go into the wilderness of your intuition.
You can't get there by bus, only by hard work and
Risk, and by not quite knowing what you're doing.
What you'll discover will be wonderful.
What you'll discover will be yourself.

♦ Alan Alda

We are in this world to learn to become wiser, more compassionate, to grow.
But if we know in advance how it will turn out in the end, how can we learn
and how can we grow?

♦ Isaac Bashevis Singer

WHATEVER GOES AROUND
COMES AROUND

This is kind of like "The Past Lives On," but not quite. Some people call the phenomenon here a "vicious circle," which the dictionary says is "a chain of events in which the solution of one difficulty creates a new problem involving increased difficulty."

If you want to keep on getting what you're getting
Keep on doing what you're doing.

♦ Les Brown

From bondage, comes spiritual faith.
  From spiritual faith, comes courage.

From courage, comes liberty.
  From liberty, comes abundance.

From abundance, comes complacency.
  From complacency, comes apathy.

From apathy, comes dependency.
  From dependency, comes bondage.

♦ Author Unknown

If we don't change our direction,
We are likely to end up where we are headed.

♦ Chinese Proverb

Wash a pig as much as you like, it goes right back to the mud.

   ♦ Russian Proverb

You got to wash the mud not the pigs.

   ♦ Clinton Terrell

There is a particularly unattractive and discouragingly common affliction called tunnel vision, which, for all the misery it caused, ought to top the job list at the World Health Organization.

Tunnel vision is a disease in which perception is restricted by ignorance and distorted by vested interest. Tunnel vision is caused by an optic fungus that multiplies when the brain is less energetic that the ego.

It is complicated by exposure to politics, when a good idea is run through the filters and compressors of ordinary tunnel vision, it not only comes out reduced in scale and value but in its new dogmatic configuration produces effects the opposite of those for which it originally was intended.

That is how the loving ideas of Jesus Christ became the sinister clichés of Christianity. That is why virtually every revolution in history has failed: the oppressed, as soon as they seize power, turn into the oppressors, resorting to totalitarian tactics to "protect the revolution."

That is why minorities seeking the abolition of prejudice become intolerant, minorities seeking peace become militant, minorities seeking equality become self-righteous, and minorities seeking liberation become hostile (a tight asshole being the first symptom of self-repression).

   ♦ Tom Robbins, "Still Life with Woodpecker"

It's all downhill till the next hill.

   ♦ Author Unknown

310

Everything has changed except our way of thinking.

◆ Albert Einstein

We have to change the way we change.

◆ ATT Slogan

New skies the exile finds, but the heart is still the same.

◆ Horace

Edges are important because they define a limitation in a frontier that tells us that we are now about to become more than we have been before. As long as one operates in the middle of things, one can never really know the nature of the medium in which one moves.

Like a mind moving on a Mobius strip of events, one's consciousness goes over the same territory again and again without ever becoming aware of the nature of awareness. In universities historians are taught to stay away from edges, to deal only with things that can be quantified, measured, and verified by other researchers.

◆ William Irwin Thompson, "The Time Falling Bodies Take To Light"

I'm including the next quote not because I accept the premise of keeping existing people in place, which I don't, but because the author and the age in which it was spoken make the comment interesting.

One of the difficulties in bringing about change in an organization is that you must do so through the persons who have been most successful in that organization, no matter how faulty the system or organization is. To such persons, you see, it is the best of all possible organizations, because look who was selected by it and look who succeeded most within it. Yet these are the very people through whom we must bring about improvements.

♦ George Washington

THAT'S GOOD ADVICE

Many of my quotes could be in this section. They are common sense, which is the best advice—sometimes. Of these quotes you could say, "Sure, any fool knows that," except we fools forget all the time.

The way out is through the door. Why is it that no one will use this exit?

   ◆ Confucius

Never insult an alligator until you have crossed the river.

   ◆ Cordell Hull, Former Secretary of State

Only when you have crossed the river, can you say the crocodile has a lump on his snout.

   ◆ Ashanti Proverb

Question: Do you think the Ashanti wise men read Hull's stuff or vice versa? I think they both stole from the Creoles of Belize: "No call haligetta big-mout till you done cross the riba."

You can't drive straight on a twisting lane.

   ◆ Russian Proverb

If there are two courses of action
You should always take the third

   ◆ Jewish Proverb

Too much of a good thing is wonderful.

   ♦ Mae West

The difference between genius and stupidity is that genius has it's limits.

   ♦ Author Unknown

To you Monday-morning quarterbacks:

If you really want to give me advice, do it on Saturday afternoon between one and four o'clock, when you've got 25 seconds to do it, between plays. Don't give me advice on Monday. I know the right thing to do on Monday.

   ♦ Alex Agase, College Football Coach

When you reach the top of the mountain, keep climbing.

   ♦ Zen Saying

We cannot know what we need to know, unless we ask what we need to ask.

   ♦ Japanese Manager

It works better if you plug it in.

   ♦ Sattinger's Law

Good advice is rarer than rubies.

   ♦ Salman Rushdie, "East, West"

A false step is not as important as the next step.

- ♦ "Ma Saison Preferee" (movie)

If you can't convince them, confuse them.

- ♦ Harry Truman

FOR SPECIAL ATTENTION:

RAINER MARIA RILKE

Pretty much everything I have from Rainer Maria Rilke could go in the "Beyond Beyond" section. He intrigues me. Rilke never said he'd give us the answers. He said love the questions and perhaps you'll live your way into the answers.

Be patient toward all that is unsolved in your heart and try to love the questions themselves, like locked rooms or books that are written in a foreign tongue.

* * *

Where I am folded in upon myself, there I am a lie.

* * *

Fame is the sum of misunderstandings that collect around a person.

* * *

The other world, the "higher" world, is this world consciously experienced.

* * *

If I don't manage to fly, someone else will.
The spirit wants only that there be flying.
As for who happens to do it,
In that he has only a passing interest.

* * *

If only we would arrange our life according
To that principle which counsels us
That we must always hold to the difficult,
Then that which now still seems to us
The most alien will become that which we
Most trust and find most faithful.

* * *

Take your well-disciplined strengths and stretch them between two opposing
    poles.
Because inside human beings is where God learns.

* * *

And now let us welcome the New Year
Full of things that have never been.

* * *

And in the silent, sometimes hardly moving times when something is
coming near, I want to be with those who know secret things, or else alone.

* * *

What we choose to fight is so tiny!
What fights with us is so great!
If only we would let ourselves be dominated
as things do by some immense storm,
we would become strong too, and not need names.

When we win it's with small things,
and the triumph itself makes us small.
What is extraordinary and eternal
does not want to be bent by us.
I mean the Angel who appeared
to the wrestlers of the Old Testament:

When the wrestler's sinews
grew long like metal strings,
he felt them under his fingers
like chords of deep music.

Whoever was beaten by this Angel
(who often simply declined the fight)
went away proud and strengthened
and great from that harsh hand,
that kneaded him as if to change his shape.
Winning does not tempt that man.
This is how he grows: by being defeated, decisively,
by constantly greater beings.

* * *

You see, I want a lot.
Perhaps I want everything:
the darkness that comes with every infinite fall
and the shivering blaze of every step up.

So many live on and want nothing,
and are raised to the rank of prince
by the slippery ease of their light judgments.

But what you love to see are faces
that do work and feel thirst.

You love most of all those who need you
as they need a crowbar on a hoe.

You have not grown old, and it is not too late
to dive into your increasing depths
where life calmly gives out its own secret.

* * *

Why, if this interval of being can be spent serenely
in the form of a laurel, slightly darker than all
other green, with tiny waves on the edges
of every leaf (like the smile of a breeze)—: why then
have to be human...?

Oh *not* because happiness *exists*,
that too-hasty profit snatched from approaching loss.
Not out of curiosity, not as practice for the heart, which
would exist in the laurel too...

But because *truly* being here is so much; because
    everything here
apparently needs us, this fleeting world, which in some
    strange way
keeps calling to us. Us, the most fleeting of all.
Once for each thing. Just once; no more. And we too,
just once. And never again. But to have been
this once, completely, even if only once:
to have been at one with the earth, seems beyond undoing.

And so we keep pressing on, trying to achieve it,
trying to hold it firmly in our simple hands,
in our overcrowded gaze, in our speechless heart.
Trying to become it.—Whom can we give it to? We
    would
hold on to it all, forever...

For when the traveler returns from the mountain-slopes
    into the valley,
he brings, not a handful of earth, unsayable to other,
    but instead
some word he has gained, some pure word, the yellow and
    blue
gentian. Perhaps we are *here* in order to say: house,
bridge, fountain, gate, pitcher, fruit-tree, window—
at most: column, tower...But to *say* them, you must
    understand,
oh to say them *more* intensely than the Things themselves

ever dreamed of existing. Isn't the secret intent
of this taciturn earth, when it forces lovers together,
that inside their boundless emotion all things may
    shudder with joy?

Praise this world to the angel, not the unsayable one,
you can't impress *him* with glorious emotion; in the
    universe
where he feels more powerfully, you are a novice. So
    show him
something simple which, formed over generations,
lives as our own, near our hand and within our gaze.
Tell him of Things. He will stand astonished; as *you*
    stood
by the rope-maker in Rome or the potter along the Nile.
Show him how happy a Thing can be, how innocent and
    ours,
how even lamenting grief purely decides to take form,
serves as a Thing, or dies into a Thing...

                    And these Things,
which live by perishing, know you are praising them;
    transient,
they look to us for deliverance: us, the most
    transient of all.
They want us to change them, utterly, in our invisible
    heart,
within—oh endlessly—within us! Whoever we may be at
    last.

Earth, isn't this what you want: to arise within us,
invisible? Isn't it your dream
to be wholly invisible someday?--O Earth: invisible!
What, if not transformation, is your urgent command?

    ♦ "Ninth Duino Elegy"

REACHING OUT

When I was running the Breakthrough Foundation and it's Youth at Risk Program I was often asked how I knew when a kid really had turned his life around. I said it was when the focus of his life shifted from "me" to reaching out to help others. Obviously, that shift in focus is relevant to all of us, not just young people in trouble.

Power means to me pretty much the same thing as freedom. By 'power' I mean human faculties exercised to the largest possible degree. So in a way, in a large sense, by power I mean individual intelligence. Now when you reach out to another person through the energy or creativity that is in you and that other person responds, you are exercising power. When you make somebody else do something against their will, to me that is not power at all, that is force, and force to me is the negation of power.

◆ Charles Reich, "Power and the Law"

Service is actually that kind of relationship in which you have a commitment to the person. Now I don't mean to the person's body or to the person's personality, but to who the other person really is. You are only as valuable as you can deal with the other person's stuff. Service is about knowing who the other person is, and being able to tolerate giving space to their garbage.

What most people do is to give space to people's quality and deal with their garbage. Actually, you should do it the other way around. Deal with who they are and give space to their garbage. Keep interacting with them as if they were God. And every time you get garbage from them, give space to the garbage and go back and interact with them as if they were God.

◆ Werner Erhard

Greek definition of happiness: The exercise of vital powers along lines of excellence and a life affording scope.

◆ Author Unknown

Everybody can be great. Because anybody can serve. You don't have to have a college degree to serve. You don't have to make your subject and verb agree to serve. You don't have to know about Plato and Aristotle to serve. You don't have to know Einstein's Theory of Relativity to serve. You don't have to know the second theory of thermodynamics in physics to serve. You only need a heart full of grace. A soul generated by love.

◆ Martin Luther King, Jr.

Every man must decide whether he will walk in the light of creative altruism or the darkness of destructive selfishness. This is the judgment. Life's most persistent and urgent question is, what are you doing for others?

◆ Martin Luther King, Jr.

Service/volunteer work is the rent that you pay for room on this earth.

◆ Attributed to both Shirley Chisholm & Mohammed Ali

We make a living by what we get,
But we make a life by what we give.

◆ Winston Churchill

Conversion to the people requires a profound rebirth. Those who undergo it must take on a new form of existence. They can no longer remain as they were.

◆ Paolo Freire

This next one is a different way of commenting on the importance of "Reaching Out." However, clearly the mood is one of disappointment (Bill Moyers was a key player in the early days of the Peace Corps) and even cynicism. I toyed with not including it because maybe Moyers was just expressing himself on a bad day. However:

The Peace Corps was born after a long season during which young Americans had been spiritually unemployed. Now, once again, a generation of Americans is tempted to live undisturbed, buying tranquillity on credit while hearts atrophy, quarantined from any great enthusiasm but private ambition.

   ♦ Bill Moyers

All that is not given is lost.

   ♦ P. Lal

A life is not important except in the impact it has on other lives.

   ♦ Jackie Robinson

There is enough for everyone's need but not enough for everyone's greed.

   ♦ Mahatma Gandhi

HEY, LOOK WHAT I DID

There's a big difference between thinking about doing something, or talking about it, and actually getting it done.

The hen is the wisest of all the animal creation. She never cackles until after the egg is laid.

♦ Abraham Lincoln

In physics the definition of work is: W=FxD, or work equals force times distance. It does not make any difference how hard you pushed against the rock; if you have not moved it, you have not done any work.

♦ Robert Behn, "Policy Analysts, Clients and Social Scientists"

Execution is the chariot of genius.

♦ William Blake

If you're resting on your laurels, you're wearing them in the wrong place.

♦ Author Unknown

Success is moving from failure to failure with no loss of enthusiasm.

♦ Winston Churchill

Nothing great was ever achieved without enthusiasm.

♦ Ralph Waldo Emerson

My grandfather told me that there are two kinds of people: those who do the work and those who take the credit. He told me to try to be in the first group; there was less competition there.

> ♦ Indira Gandhi

The essence of action is accomplishment. To accomplish means to unfold something into the fullness of its essence, to lead it forth into this fullness.

> ♦ Martin Heidegger, "Letter on Humanism"

I never notice what has been done. I only see what remains to be done.

> ♦ Madame Marie Curie

Thunder is good, thunder is impressive;
but it is lightning that does the work.

> ♦ Mark Twain

If you expect to see the final results of your work, you have not asked a big enough question.

> ♦ I. F. Stone

I'd been chasing the game. Tonight I let it come to me.

> ♦ Michael Jordan (after returning to basketball and playing well for the first time)

You can't make an omelet without breaking eggs.

> ♦ Author Unknown

Prayer without action is no prayer at all. You have to do your work as if everything depends on you, then leave the rest to God.

♦ Mother Teresa

I have not the shadow of a doubt that any man or woman can achieve what I have, if he or she would make the same effort and cultivate the same hope and faith.

What is faith worth if it is not translated into action?

♦ Mahatma Gandhi

It appears the Mahatma and the Mother have some wisdom in common.

The problem in my life and other people's lives is not absence of knowing what to do but the absence of doing it.

♦ Peter Drucker

The highest reward for a person's toil is not what they get for it, but what they become by it.

♦ John Ruskin

Things may come to those who wait but only the things left by those who hustle.

♦ Abraham Lincoln

It's probably true that hard work never killed anyone, but I figure why take the chance.

♦ Ronald Reagan

When nothing seems to help, I go and look at a stonecutter hammering away at his rock perhaps a hundred times without as much as a crack showing in it. Yet at the hundred and first blow it will split in two, and I know it was not that blow that did it but all that had gone before.

♦ Jacob Riis

Don't worry about the horse being blind. Load up the wagon.

♦ John Madden

Brakes stop wheels. Tires stop the car.

♦ Goodyear Tire Commercial

If I know I should win [the Tony Award] I don't have to.

♦ Elaine Strich, Actress

The perfect man of action is the suicide.

♦ William Carlos Williams

VISION

Creating a vision is both exciting and frightening. It's like creating a new future that does not yet exist and would not become real without us. Even with a vision, though, we are still at risk. Our vision does not tell us what to do. It does not tell us how to act. It does not tell us what's right and wrong.

A vision gives us power. It gives us a place to stand, a place to come from. It is also like a great coach or mentor or compass: it keeps us straight by letting us know if we're on track in turning what we say we are committed to into reality.

The real question is not how do you get what you want, but what do you really want.

♦ Bob Shaw

There is nothing more difficult to take in hand, more perilous to conduct, or more uncertain in its success, than to take the lead in the introduction of a new order of things.

♦ Niccolo Machiavelli

Herzl was like all great visionaries. He could see the unseen and overlook the obvious.

♦ Amos Elon

Those who dream by night in the dusty recesses of their minds,
Wake in the day to find that all was but vanity;
But the dreamers of the day are dangerous men,
For they may act their dream with open eyes and make it possible.

♦ T.E. Lawrence

Gods are amused when the busy river condemns the cloud as an impractical dream.

   ♦ Rabindranath Tagore

He seemed to win by a constant renewal of effort, in which he refused to sink either into placid acceptance of the world, or into self-contained satisfaction with his vision.

   ♦ Walter Lippmann on H.G. Wells

Vision is having an acute sense of the possible. It is seeing what others don't see.

   ♦ Shearson/Lehman/American Express

I loved you so much I drew these hoards of men into my hands and wrote my will across the sky in stars, to earn you freedom.

   ♦ T.E. Lawrence

History is an exact science
Vision is an uncertain challenge

   ♦ Author Unknown

We are looking for an idea large enough to be afraid of again.

   ♦ Tyrone Guthrie

This is what we need. Not just stopping things. Not just less of things. People need something positive to work for. They need a vision...they need more than to be scolded, more than to be made to feel stupid and guilty. They need more than a vision of doom. They need a vision of the world and of themselves that inspires them.

♦ Daniel Quinn, "Ishmael"

Mahatma Gandhi said that when you are working to create social change, to create a new vision, there are inevitably five phases you will go through with respect to your work and other people:

First, when you begin your work, people react with INDIFFERENCE. That is, they won't even ask where you are going or what you are doing. Just INDIFFERENCE.

The second stage you'll encounter, if you keep on going, is RIDICULE. People will ask, "Do you think you're out to save the world?" They will lay their skepticism and cynicism on you.

The third phase you'll encounter is ABUSE. People will try to take advantage of you and your work; perhaps they'll try to undo what you've done.

Next, if you are sturdy and strong and keep on going, people will try to OPPRESS you. Maybe they'll try to stop your work legally. Maybe they'll try to kill you.

But if you keep on going and remain balanced and follow your vision, what will happen is that people will start to RESPECT you.

This is actually the most dangerous phase of all, because it is at this phase that you stand to lose your way!

♦ A.T. Ariyaratne

My idealism is the realism of tomorrow.

♦ Jawaharlal Nehru

A strong imagination begets the event.

♦ Montaigne

Every movement of infinity comes about by passion, and no reflection can bring a movement about. What our age lacks is not a reflection, but passion.

♦ Soren Kierkegaard

I LOVE YOU

Love is perfect kindness.
Love is what the eyes have made welcome to the heart.

> ◆ Joseph Campbell

As many husband has discovered to his regret, to love you have to pay attention.

> ◆ Author Unknown

The opposite of love is not hate; it is indifference.

> ◆ Elie Wiesel

A different kind of love:

It's the slavery of attachment that is hell, not the things themselves that we are attached to. It's a grave error to imagine that by giving up the object of our attachment we become free from the force of attachment itself.

"The love of money is the root of all evil," Alyssa whispered.

"It must be that," I added. "It's not the money, it's the love that is the problem."

> ◆ Jacob Needleman, "Money & the Meaning of Life"

To him in whom love dwells, the whole world is but one family.

> ◆ Buddha

Love doesn't make the world go 'round.
Love is what makes the ride worthwhile.

♦ Franklin P. Jones

The music in my heart I bore
Long after it was heard no more.

♦ William Wordsworth

Love adds a precious seeing to the eye.

♦ William Shakespeare

Nobody has ever measured, even poets, how much a heart can hold.

♦ Zelda Fitzgerald

Nothing matters but the quality of the affection—
In the end—that has carved the trace in the mind
Dove sta memoria

♦ Ezra Pound, "Canto LXXVI"

The truth is that there is only one terminal dignity—love. And the story of a love is not important—what is important is that one is capable of love. It is perhaps the only glimpse we are permitted of eternity.

♦ Helen Hayes

I love you because of who you are—and who I am when I am with you.

♦ Franklin McCormick

And:

She laughed, not because she missed him, but because she missed the person she had been with him.

    ♦ David Grossman, "The Book of Intimate Grammar"

For new lovers, the heart is an organ on fire.

    ♦ Michael Ondaatje, "The English Patient"

Strange shapes and void afflict the soul
And shadow to the eye
A world on fire while smoke seas roll
And lightnings rend the sky

The moon shall be as blood the sun
Black as a thunder cloud
The stars shall turn to blue and dun
And heaven by darkness bowed
Shall make sun dark and give no day
When stars like skys shall be
When heaven and earth shall pass away
Wilt thou Remember me

    ♦ John Clare

Love took up the harp of life
And smote on all the chords with might;
Smote the chord of Self which, trembling,
Passed in music out of sight.

    ♦ Alfred Lord Tennyson, "Locksley Hall"

TO THINE OWN SELF BE TRUE

From Shakespeare's "Hamlet":

This above all: to thine own self be true,
And it must follow, as the night the day,
Thou canst not then be false to any man.

Living up to my personal values and ideals, and maintaining them in the face of life, is difficult. When I am most proud of myself, or when I am inspired by another, it usually has something to do with integrity of self, being true to oneself. That kind of integrity cannot be imposed. It is created by me and freely chosen by me. It allows me to express who I really am.

All deep, earnest thinking is but the intrepid effort of the soul to keep the open independence of her seas. While the wildest winds of heaven and earth conspire to cast her upon the treacherous slavish shore.

♦ Herman Melville, "Moby Dick"

We are what we pretend to be, so we must be careful what we pretend to be.

♦ Kurt Vonnegut

In India, "namaste" is a traditional greeting. It is "hello," "goodbye," and more:

Namaste means I honor the place in you where the entire universe resides. I honor the place in you of love, of light, of truth, of peace. I honor the place within you where if you are in that place in you and I am in that place in me, there is only one of us.

♦ Author Unknown

The most important thing in a man is not what he knows, but what he is.

♦ Narcisso Yepes

To the as-yet-unborn, to all innocent wisps of undifferentiated nothingness:
Watch out for life.

I have caught life. I have come down with life, I was a wisp of undifferentiated nothingness, and then a little peephole opened quite suddenly. Light and sound poured in. Voices began to describe me and my surroundings. Nothing they said could be appealed. They said I was a boy named Rudolph Waltz, and that was that. They said this year was 1932, and that was that. They said I was in Midland City, Ohio, and that was that.

They never shut up. Year after year they piled detail upon detail. They do it still. You know what they say now? They say the year is 1982, and that I am fifty years old. Blah-blah-blah.

♦ Kurt Vonnegut, "Dead Eye Dick"

If you're a rooster, crow; if you're a hen, shut up and lay eggs.

♦ Russian Proverb

We're people in a book who don't always know what the author wants.

♦ Julian Green

Obviously, these next two could be in "Heroes." Hero, it occurs to me, is not a bad characterization for us when we are true to ourselves:

To be a hero is finally to embrace the person we really are, and to live in the world that this acceptance creates all around us.

♦ Thomas Van Nortwick

340

Success rests with having the courage and endurance, and above all, the will to become the person you are, however peculiar that may be. Then, you can say, I have found my hero and he is me.

    ◆ George Sheehan

Fear is the mind-killer. Fear is the little death that brings total obliteration. I will face my fear. I will permit it to pass over me and through me. And when it has gone past me I will turn to see fear's path. Where the fear has gone there will be nothing. Only I will remain.

    ◆ Frank Herbert, "Dune"

I don't like work, no man does, but I find I like what is in work—the chance to find yourself. Your own reality, for yourself, not for others—what no other man can ever know.

    ◆ Joseph Conrad, "Heart of Darkness"

How queer everything is today! And yesterday things went on just as usual. I wonder if I've been changed in the night? Let me think: WAS I the same when I got up this morning? I almost think I can remember feeling a little different. But if I'm not the same, the next question is, "Who in the world am I?" Ah, that's the great puzzle!

    ◆ Lewis Carroll, "Alice in Wonderland"

I have often thought that the best way to define a man's character would be to seek out the particular mental or moral attitude in which, when it came upon him, he felt himself most deeply and intensively active and alive. At such moments, there is a voice inside which speaks and says, "This is the real me."

    ◆ William James, "Letters of William James"

Whenever you think or you believe or you know, you are a lot of other people: But the moment you are being, you're being nobody but yourself.

♦ e.e. cummings

Let each of you find where your chance for greatness lies.

♦ "Chariots of Fire" (movie)

As a man's real power grows and his knowledge widens, ever the way he can follow grows narrower: Until at last he chooses nothing, but does only and wholly what he must do.

♦ Ursula le Guin, "A Wizard of Earthsea"

Our deepest fear is not that we are inadequate. Our deepest fear is that we are powerful beyond measure. It is our light, not our darkness, that most frightens us.

We ask ourselves, "Who am I to be brilliant, gorgeous, talented, and fabulous?" Actually, who are you *not* to be? You are a child of God; your playing small doesn't serve the world. There is nothing enlightened about shrinking so that other people won't feel insecure around you.

We were born to make manifest the glory of God within us. It is not just in some of us, it is in *everyone* and as we let our own light shine, we unconsciously give other people permission to do the same.

As we are liberated from our own fear, our presence automatically liberates others.

♦ Nelson Mandela, Inaugural Address, 1995

You reach a certain age where you should stop waiting for the man you're gonna become. You better start being the man you want to be.

> ♦ Bruce Springsteen

In the coming world, they will not ask me: "Why were you not Moses or Akiba or Abraham?" They will ask me "Why were you not Zusya?"

> ♦ Rabbi Zusya

How long can you wear a mask before your face begins to conform to it?

> ♦ Author Unknown

I yam what I yam an' that's what I yam.

> ♦ Popeye the Sailor Man

We are too late for the Gods, too early for being. Being's poem just begun is man.

> ♦ Martin Heidegger

Two roads diverged in a wood, and I—
I took the one less traveled by,
And that has made all the difference.

> ♦ Robert Frost, "The Road Not Taken"

We have our secrets and our needs to confess. We may remember how, in childhood, adults were able at first to look right through us, and into us, and what an accomplishment it was when we, in fear and trembling, could tell our first lie, and make, for ourselves, the discovery that we are irredeemably alone in certain respects, and know that within the territory of ourselves, there can be only our footprints.

♦ R.D. Laing, "The Divided Self"

Index

9 780965 308618